Robert E. Lee

A LIPPER™/VIKING BOOK

ROY BLOUNT, JR.

Robert E. Lee

A Penguin Life

A LIPPER™/VIKING BOOK

VIKING
Published by the Penguin Group
Penguin Putnam Inc., 375 Hudson Street, New York, New York 10014, U.S.A.
Penguin Books Ltd, 80 Strand, London WC2R 0RL, England
Penguin Books Australia Ltd, 250 Camberwell Road, Camberwell,
Victoria 3124, Australia
Penguin Books Canada Ltd, 10 Alcorn Avenue
Toronto, Ontario, Canada M4V 3B2
Penguin Books India (P) Ltd, 11 Community Centre, Panchsheel Park,
New Delhi–110 017, India
Penguin Books (N.Z.) Ltd, Cnr Rosedale and Airborne Roads, Albany,
Auckland, New Zealand
Penguin Books (South Africa) (Pty) Ltd, 24 Sturdee Avenue,
Rosebank, Johannesburg 2196, South Africa

Penguin Books Ltd, Registered Offices:
Harmondsworth, Middlesex, England

First published in 2003 by Viking Penguin,
a member of Penguin Putnam Inc.

1   3   5   7   9   10   8   6   4   2

LIBRARY OF CONGRESS CATALOGING-IN-PUBLICATION DATA
Blount, Roy.
Robert E. Lee: a Penguin life / Roy Blount, Jr.
p.   cm.–(Penguin lives series)
Includes bibliographical references. (p.   )
ISBN 0-670-03220-4
1. Lee, Robert E. (Robert Edward), 1807–1870. 2. Generals–
Confederate States of America–Biography. 3. Confederate States of America.
Army–Biography. 4. United States–History–Civil War, 1861–1865–
Campaigns. I. Title. II. Series.
E467.1.L4 B58 2003
973.7'3'092–dc21
[B]   2002032423

This book is printed on acid-free paper. ∞

Printed in the United States of America
Set in Berthold Garamond   Designed by Francesca Belanger

CONTENTS

Robert E. Lee   1

APPENDIX I. *Speculation*   165

APPENDIX II. *Lee's Humor*   189

APPENDIX III. *Lee's Attitude Toward Slavery*   197

BIBLIOGRAPHY   207

Robert E. Lee

CHAPTER ONE

It is well that war is so terrible, or we should grow too fond of it.
—Robert E. Lee, at Fredericksburg

Shut up, Bobby Lee. It's no real pleasure in life.
—The Misfit, in Flannery O'Connor's
"A Good Man Is Hard to Find"

IN HIS DASHING (if sometimes depressive) antebellum prime, he may have been the most beautiful person in America, a sort of precursor-cross between England's Cary Grant and Virginia's Randolph Scott. He was in his element gossiping with belles about their beaux at balls. In theaters of grinding, hellish human carnage he kept a pet hen for company. He had tiny feet that he loved his children to tickle. None of these things seems to fit, for if ever there was a grave American icon, it is Robert Edward Lee—hero of the Confederacy in the American Civil War, a unifying national figure for a century or so thereafter, and currently a symbol of nobility to some, of slavery to others.

1

After Lee's death in 1870, Frederick Douglass, the former fugitive slave who had become the nation's most prominent African American, wrote, "We can scarcely take up a newspaper . . . that is not filled with *nauseating* flatteries" of Lee, from which "it would seem . . . that the soldier who kills the most men in battle, even in a bad cause, is the greatest Christian, and entitled to the highest place in heaven." Two years later one of Lee's ex-generals, Jubal A. Early, apotheosized his late commander as follows: "Our beloved Chief stands, like some lofty column which rears its head among the highest, in grandeur, simple, pure and sublime."

In 1907 President Theodore Roosevelt expressed mainstream American sentiment in a letter to the Committee of Arrangement for the Celebration of the Hundredth Anniversary of Lee's birth:

> General Lee has left us the memory, not merely of his extraordinary skill as a General, his dauntless courage and high leadership . . . but also of that serene greatness of soul characteristic of those who most readily recognize the obligations of civic duty. . . . He stood that hardest of all strains, the strain of bearing himself well through the gray evening of failure; and therefore out of what seemed failure he helped to build the wonderful and mighty triumph of our national life, in which all his countrymen, north and south, share.

Teddy Roosevelt, Gen. Douglas MacArthur, and President Harry S. Truman had at least three things in common with Lee: They were all brave soldiers, staunch leaders of men, and, in no pejorative sense, mama's boys. Both Truman and

MacArthur were adjured by their strong-minded mothers to grow up just like Robert E. Lee, and they never stopped taking that charge to heart.

When a white mob tried to prevent the integration of public schools in Little Rock, Arkansas, in 1957, Robert Penn Warren wrote, "Can the man howling in the mob imagine General R. E. Lee, CSA, shaking hands with Orval Faubus, governor of Arkansas?" Certainly not—Lee was too fine. But at the turn of the twenty-first century, a portrait of Lee on the James River floodwall in Richmond, Virginia, was defaced, restored, denounced by the National Association for the Advancement of Colored People, and defended by white supremacist David Duke. U.S. Attorney General–designate John Ashcroft was widely disparaged for having called Lee a "patriot." "We've got to stand up and speak in this respect," Ashcroft had written, "or else we'll be taught that [Lee and other Confederate leaders] were giving their lives, subscribing their sacred fortunes and their honor to some perverted agenda."

One thing that can be said for Lee is that he would have welcomed none of these pronouncements. If the self-effacing patrician could have known that his face would live on for so long as a quasi-religious, recurrently divisive symbol, it might have made him moan, as he did after sending thousands of men to be cut to ribbons at Gettysburg, "Too bad! *Too bad!* OH! TOO BAD!" He was one of the few great men of whom it can be said that his sense of honor was rooted in genuine— if in fact far from simple or serene—humility. The most sublime word, Lee said, was "duty." In 1860 he wrote to Robert E. Lee Jr., who was starting college:

You must be frank in the world, frankness is the child of honesty and courage. Say just what you mean to do on every occasion, and take it for granted you mean to do right. . . . Never do anything wrong to make a friend or keep one; the man who requires you to do so, is dearly purchased at a sacrifice. Deal kindly, but firmly with all your classmates; you will find it the policy which wears best. Above all do not appear to others what you are not.

Did he speak in such tones to *himself*? He was the last avatar, wrote Edmund Wilson approvingly, of "classical antique virtue, at once aristocratic and republican." But he was also a man. And isn't it true, as Montgomery Clift said in the role of Robert E. Lee Prewitt in *From Here to Eternity*, "Ain't nothin the matter with a soldier that ain't the matter with everybody else"?

We may think we know Lee because we have a mental image: gray. Not only the uniform, the mythic horse, the hair and beard, but the resignation with which he accepted dreary burdens that offered "neither pleasure nor advantage": in particular, the Confederacy, a cause of which he took a dim view until he went to war for it. He did not see right and wrong in tones of gray, and yet his moralizing could generate a fog, as in a letter from the front to his invalid wife: "You must endeavour to enjoy the pleasure of doing good. That is all that makes life valuable." All right. But then he adds: "When I measure my own by that standard I am filled with confusion and despair."

His own hand probably never drew human blood nor fired a shot in anger, and his only Civil War wound was a faint scratch on the cheek from a sharpshooter's bullet, but many thousands of men died quite horribly in battles where he was the dominant–fiery–spirit, and most of the casualties were on the other side. If we take as a given Lee's granitic conviction that everything is God's will, however, he was born to lose.

He was usually kinder than most great men. But in even the most sympathetic versions of his life story he comes across as a bit of a stick–certainly compared with his scruffy nemesis, Ulysses S. Grant; his zany, ferocious "right arm," Stonewall Jackson; and the dashing "eyes" of his army, Jeb Stuart. For these men, the Civil War was just the ticket. Lee, however, has come down in history as too fine for the bloodbath of 1861–65. As an icon he has enabled Americans of the South and also of the North to feel that somehow the American family was too decent to have brought upon itself four years of domestic carnage. To efface the squalor and horror of the war we have the image of Abraham Lincoln freeing the slaves, and we have the image of Robert E. Lee nobly putting down his sword and standing selflessly for reconciliation. Both of those images have undergone reassessment–for many contemporary Americans, Lee is at best the moral equivalent of Hitler's brilliant field marshal Erwin Rommel (who, however, turned against Hitler, as Lee never did against Jefferson Davis, who, to be sure, was no Hitler)–but they haven't gone away.

Can we recast Lee in terms more edifying in this century?

One problem is that Lee's life didn't fit him. He appears to have been too fine for his childhood, for his education, for his profession, for his marriage, and for the Confederacy. Not according to him. According to him, he was not fine enough. For all his audacity on the battlefield, he accepted rather passively one raw deal after another, bending over backward for everyone from Jefferson Davis to James McNeill Whistler's mother.

By what can we know him? The works of a general are battles, campaigns, and usually memoirs. The engagements of the Civil War shape up more as bloody muddles than as commanders' chess games. For a long time during the war "Old Bobbie Lee," as he was referred to worshipfully by his troops and nervously by the foe, had the greatly superior Union forces spooked, but a century and a third of analysis and counteranalysis has resulted in no core consensus as to the genius or the folly of his generalship. And he wrote no memoir. He wrote personal letters—a discordant mix of flirtation, joshing, lyrical touches, and stern religious adjuration—and he wrote official dispatches that are so impersonal and (generally) unself-serving as to seem above the fray. He also wrote one strange parable, which had come to him in a dream.

Grant finally wore down Lee's ingenious military defenses, but he didn't crack his facade: There at the end stood Lee at Appomattox, too fine to represent defeat. In 1959, two years after citing Lee as a touchstone, Robert Penn Warren—who had written a biography of John Brown and a novel whose central character was inspired by Huey Long—grumbled, "Who cares about Robert E. Lee? Now, there's a man who's smooth as an egg. Turn him around, this primordial perfection: you see, he has no story. You can't just say what a wonderful man he was, and that you know he had some chaotic something inside because he's human but you can't get at it."

Maybe in this century, after monumentalism has given way to chaos theory and obsession with the self, we can at last figure out how to care humanly about the self that Robert E. Lee was at such pains to deny. The only way to get inside him, perhaps, is by edging fractally around the record of his life to find spots where he comes through; by holding up next to him some of the fully realized characters—Grant, Jackson, Stuart, his father (Light-Horse Harry Lee), John Brown—with whom he interacted; and by subjecting to contemporary skepticism certain concepts—honor, "gradual emancipation," divine will—upon which he unreflectively founded his identity.

Then there are minor but provocative matters like his feet, a peculiar instance of misspelling, his pet hen, his enigmatic "Pussyism" joke. For all that he tends to bring out a certain solemnity, even in discussions of his humor, he was capable of larky jocularity in the oddest connections and the darkest of times. If in considering his sad life we strive for too consistent a tone, we miss some of its jangly resonance. As he would say to his children when he was at his most intimate with them, "No tickling, no story."

He wasn't always gray. Until war aged him dramatically his sharp dark brown eyes were complemented by black hair ("ebon and abundant," as his doting biographer Douglas Southall Freeman puts it, "with a wave that a woman might have envied"), a robust black mustache, a strong full mouth and chin unobscured by any beard, and dark mercurial brows. He was not one to hide his looks under a bushel. His heart, on the other hand . . . "The heart, he kept locked away," as Stephen Vincent Benét proclaimed in *John Brown's Body*, "from all the picklocks of biographers." Accounts by people who knew him give the impression that no one knew his whole heart, even before it was broken by the war. Perhaps it broke many years before the war. "You know she is like her papa, always wanting something," he wrote about one of his daughters. The great Southern diarist of his day, Mary Chesnut, tells us that when a lady teased him about his ambitions, "[h]e remonstrated—said his tastes were of the simplest. He only wanted a Virginia farm—no end of cream and fresh butter—and fried chicken. Not one fried chicken or two—but unlimited fried chicken." Just before Lee's surrender at Appomattox, one of his nephews found him in the field, "very grave and tired," carrying around a fried chicken leg wrapped in a piece of bread, which a Virginia countrywoman had pressed upon him but for which he couldn't muster any hunger.

In 1960 Robert Penn Warren was trying, unsuccessfully, to write an essay about Lee's decision to side with the Confederacy. "I do hope you can manage [it]," Warren's friend Cleanth Brooks wrote to him. Brooks was a fellow Southerner and a prime mover along with Warren in the so-called New Criticism, which concentrated on literature's intrinsic texture rather than its political and biographical ramifications, and he seemed to want Lee's texture to be enough. "You are right: that shouldn't fall into the wrong hands," Brooks went on. "I don't want to see a Lee throwing in his lot with the Confederacy because of an Oedipus complex, for instance." Well, why not? What is so fine about Lee that he is exempt from whatever sifter a given age may employ to sort out personality? It is too late for Freud now, but not for psychologizing. Item: A recent study found boys brought up in "mother-only households" to be disproportionately at risk for major depressive disorders. (See Appendix I.)

A boy who grows up with no father but one who is absent and discredited may lack certain tones of voice, may develop alternative modes of authority. Of the precious few memories Robert E. Lee can have had of his prodigal father coming home, the most vivid, we may assume, was of a broken, grotesquely swollen figure hobbling up the front walk, head swathed in bandages. A mob of patriots, as they saw themselves, had beaten Henry "Light-Horse Harry" Lee, hero of the Revolution, very nearly to death. They had jabbed him with pocketknives and dripped candle wax into his eyes in attempts to make sure he *was* dead. They had slashed his face wide open in trying to cut off his nose. He had been defending a newspaper's right to oppose a war.

It was 1812. Robert was five years old.

On his father's side, Lee's family was among Virginia's and therefore the nation's most distinguished. Four of his father's cousins had been prominent members of the Continental Congress—so prominent, indeed, that other first families expressed resentment that the Lees were hogging the Revolution.

Henry, the scion who was to become Light-Horse Harry, was born in 1756. As a young a man he was always cheerful, ever gallant toward the ladies, a hell of a fellow among the fellows, given to flights of wild and biting humor, fiercely opinionated, and able to quote Alexander Pope at length from memory. He graduated from Princeton at nineteen, joined the Continental Army at twenty as a captain of dragoons, and impressed Gen. Charles Lee, no very direct relation, as having "come out of his mother's womb a soldier."

Though physically rather slight and facially rather plump, Harry looked fine on a horse and rode like the cavalier he was by birth. As he rose in rank and independence to command Lee's light cavalry and then Lee's legion of cavalry and infantry, he held the intense loyalty of his troops by combining strict discipline, bold stratagems, constant readiness to ride, and prudent preparation, including attention to hygiene: "I never saw one of his men in the general hospital," said an army surgeon. Every one of his cavalrymen eventually carried a sword taken personally from an enemy. When one of his men went over to the British, Harry captured him, hanged him, beheaded him, and proudly sent the head and neck with the rope still around it to his commander and hero, George Washington, who, however, was appalled.

Primarily Harry was no major-engagement man but a gadfly, a leader of freelance forays against superior forces. Once he and a lieutenant, an ensign, and fifty-nine enlisted men attacked a full battalion of more than two hundred redcoats and killed or captured more than a third of them, while suffering only one slight wound among themselves.

Sometimes eleven Oneida warriors, on their own horses, joined his cavalry troop for the sport of the thing. Harry learned their language and sat them down to dine in the field with him and the other officers, from chinaware and sterling cups. Without the medicines, elixirs, and food Harry Lee's raiders captured from the enemy, Washington's army would not likely have survived the harrowing winter encampment of 1777–78 at Valley Forge, during which men were reduced to eating their boots. Washington became his patron and close friend.

At length Sir William Howe sent a full regiment of cavalry, more than three hundred men, to capture Lee dead or alive. They cornered him in a farmhouse. Harry and a handful of his men took their shots carefully enough to repulse the British three times. Then Harry ran outside, looked into the distance, and whooped, "Here comes our infantry! We'll have them all!" Although these reinforcements were imaginary, the British fled, leaving scores of dead and wounded behind. Again, only one of Harry's men was wounded, and he but slightly.

This was one of several hairbreadth escapes Harry made as he plagued the British in Virginia and North Carolina under Nathanael Greene and in South Carolina alongside Francis Marion, "the Swamp Fox." Then, with the war nearly over, Harry decided he was underappreciated, so he impulsively resigned from the army.

That was a mistake. In 1785, however, Harry was elected to the Second Continental Congress. In 1788 he helped lead the fight in Virginia to ratify the U.S. Constitution. Ironically, in light of later developments, it was Harry who offered the most notable defense of the phrase "We, the people." Patrick Henry insisted that it should be "We, the states," but

Harry said, "This system is submitted to the people for their consideration because on them it is to operate, if adopted. It is not binding on the people until it becomes their act."

In 1791 Harry was elected governor of Virginia. In 1794 Washington put him in command of the troops that bloodlessly put down the Whiskey Rebellion (farmers protesting an excise tax) in western Pennsylvania. In 1799 he was elected to the U.S. Congress, where he famously eulogized Washington as "first in war, first in peace, and first in the hearts of his countrymen."

By that time, however, he had swapped Washington five thousand acres of real estate for a horse named Magnolia. That was just another of his impulsive acts. He had also tried to repay a loan from Washington with property to which he lacked title. That was much worse. It was a betrayal of his hero and a sign of personal disorder that Harry would project onto the common people. Harry's bad head for business, and his growing contempt for the general public, would lead him at last into a trap he couldn't escape.

In 1819 Harry's defense of "We, the people" would serve as the touchstone for Chief Justice John Marshall's ruling that "[t]he government proceeds directly from the people . . . and is declared to be ordained 'in order to form a more perfect union.' . . . The assent of the States . . . is implied. . . . But the people were at perfect liberty to accept or reject it; and their act was final. . . . The government of the Union, then, . . . is emphatically and truly a government of the people." As the concept of "the people" has evolved over the years—to include people without property, freed slaves, women, black people denied civil rights—the Constitution has remained flexible enough, over more than two centuries, to support the gradually strengthening notion of American liberty and inclusiveness.

In the nineteenth century, however, Harry lost his own flexibility, which had so dazzled the redcoats. His fast and loose speculation in hundreds of thousands of the new nation's acres went sour. One of his creditors defaulted on a huge loan. Harry was reduced to chicanery. He withheld his married daughter's dowry, gave a bad check to a friend. When in 1808 he wrote to his old college chum James Madison, now secretary of state, asking to be sent abroad, Madison did not respond. Mortified, in ill health, with all his stratagems exhausted, Harry spent a year in debtors' prison, where he wrote his war memoirs, which are energetic.

In the memoirs Harry proclaimed a determination to revive the Federalist glory, symbolized by the iconic Washington, which he felt had been obliterated by Jeffersonian democracy. He accused the Republicans, as the relatively populist Jeffersonians were known, of vitiating the central government and the military, of falsely linking Federalism with monarchism (Republicans had been known to express suspicions that the Federalists wanted to make Washington king), and of destroying what should have been a boom economy. Harry extolled Washington, exaggerated his own role—considerable though it had been—in defending the southern colonies, and strongly implied that Thomas Jefferson, as wartime governor of Virginia, had shown cowardice by briefly withdrawing from Richmond under British invasion. The memoir vexed Jefferson until his dying days, but it did not sell. In 1809 Harry was out of prison, but deep in a financial and psychological hole.

When Harry was a young bachelor, his father had asked him why he never visited brothels. He had replied, "I am ever sensible of the good name this family enjoys in the county, sir." Now the disorder of his own affairs and his gift for making prominent enemies had sullied that name. Harry turned his shame and anxiety outward: Indulgence of the masses was leading to anarchy, which would undo the Revolution and give way to monarchy. When he'd defended "We, the people," he'd actually meant "We, the gentlemen." He was no longer a gentleman himself, for all intents and purposes, and someone had to be blamed.

Jefferson and Madison, Harry argued, were forcing the nation into a disastrous war with Great Britain. Alexander Hanson of Baltimore, publisher of a Federalist newspaper, was of the same opinion, and after what is now known as the (as it turned out, quite nearly disastrous) War of 1812 was declared, Hanson attacked the Republicans' war inflammatorily. Baltimore was a Republican town, not a pacifist one. A mob stormed the newspaper plant and tore the whole building down. Hanson left town but returned with a defense force of armed Federalist partisans. Harry, who had been a friend of Hanson's father, came to Baltimore and took command.

A mob surrounded the newspaper's new office, so threateningly that Lee, over Hanson's protests, persuaded the Federalists to let themselves be locked up in jail—with pistols—for their safety. Then the mob stormed the jail. Loath to die at the hands of people such as these, Lee suggested that the Federalists shoot each other, honorably. He was voted down. When the rabble burst in, Harry denounced them as "base villains" until they clubbed and strangled him insensible. The mob killed one of the Federalists (the mob called them Tories) and were content in the belief that they had killed eight others—including Lee.

He wasn't dead (and the war was indeed ill advised), but he was defaced. A man who saw him the next day said, "Lee was black as a negro." He would spend the rest of his days in physical misery from injuries, external and internal, inflicted by the mob.

He was fifty-eight when Robert saw him return home broken. Harry had lost his fortune and lots of other people's money, as well as all of his horses. He and his household—his second wife, Ann Carter Lee, and their five surviving children, of whom Robert was the next to last—had departed the Lee ancestral home, the mansion called Stratford, where Robert was born, for a smaller rented house in Alexandria. Ann had always preferred *her* ancestral home at Shirley, Virginia, where she and the children spent so much time that Robert probably had not seen much of his father even when he wasn't in jail. Harry's self-dramatizing ways were still engaging enough, apparently, that his family continued to find him dashing, or encouraged him to believe that they did, but now that sentiment was limited—and tenuously—to that household.

Under the conditions of bankruptcy that obtained in those days, Harry was still liable for his debts. Some months after being brought back home, he jumped a personal-appearance bail—to the dismay of his brother, Edmund, who had posted a sizable bond—and wangled passage, with pitying help from President James Monroe, to the West Indies.

To his family he sent no money (Ann made do with the income from her inheritance), but long letters full of advice that may remind us of Shakespeare's stuffy Polonius—stressing honor, duty, the memory of Washington, and avoidance of debt. He never wrote directly to Robert, but did refer to him once in a letter to his older brother Carter: "Robert was always good, and will be confirmed in his happy turn of mind by his everwatchful and affectionate mother. Does he strengthen his native tendency?" In 1818, after five years away, Harry headed home to die, but got only as far as Cumberland Island, Georgia, where he was buried. Robert was eleven.

Robert had his father's nose, but from the one painting that is presumed to be a portrait of Ann Hill Carter Lee, we can infer that he got his mother's dark eyes. The hair too; the beauty. It may not be fanciful to see in her something of Vivien Leigh's Scarlett, repressed. Ann was tall for a woman of the time, delicate, however, and said to have "grave humor," no examples of which survive except perhaps as reflected by Robert. The Carters were nearly as great a Virginia family as the Lees. Ann's father, Charles—who had twenty-one children in all—was as close a friend of George Washington as Harry, and much wealthier. He had not been tempted by land speculation. Ann fell in love with Harry the widower, seventeen years her senior, while he was courting her more vivacious cousin Maria, who rejected him as a fortune hunter and urged her friend Ann to do the same—so did her parents, strenuously—when Harry turned his attentions to her without missing a beat. Ever gentle but resolute, Ann followed her heart. A wedding gift was a locket containing a portrait of the giver, inscribed, "George Washington to his dear Ann."

Harry described Ann once by quoting from Alexander Pope:

> So unaffected, so composed a mind,
> So firm, yet soft, so strong, yet so refined,
> Heaven as its purest gold, by tortures toy'd.

The principal torture was Harry. According to a relative, Ann realized within weeks of her wedding that Harry did not love her. Her dowry was soon gone. Reminders of the late first wife, in particular her shrouded harp and her spiteful daughter Lucy, filled the house. The Carters heard that Harry was seeing other women. Ann ailed and was lonely. But she didn't complain, even to friends, and she bore Harry six children, the first of whom died in infancy and the fifth of whom, she confessed to a friend, she did not want. That was Robert. Her pregnancy with him was particularly stressful. Her father died, putting her inheritance in trust "free from the claim, demand, let, hindrance or molestation of her husband . . . or his creditors," and her sister was dying. Her children all got sick. Henry refused to provide her with a carriage. Her letters betray no sign of bitterness.

She was a saint. And Robert Edward, named for two of

her brothers, loved her. As a father figure he had George Washington, long dead. With his mother and his siblings, after the move to Alexandria, he often visited Arlington House, the home of the late Father of Our Country's adopted son, George Washington Parke Custis, who told the children stories about Washington and showed them his stepfather's pistols, his outsize coats, the bed he died in. Custis's daughter, the delicate Mary Anne Custis, was Robert's playmate.

If Robert had come from *his* mother's womb a soldier, he was not one at her knee. Another soldier was not what she needed. Where Harry was brash and profligate, Robert under his mother's influence grew up unnaturally self-controlled. He was a born horseman, to be sure, and his frame was sturdier than his father's, his face stronger. He relished swimming in the Potomac, shooting partridges and ducks, and outfoxing foxhunters by following the hounds on foot and taking clever shortcuts so that when the mounted hunters reached the kill, young Robert was there already. Anticipation, sense of terrain, outlandish surprise: the essentials eventually of his generalship.

Ann Carter Lee needed someone to talk to, and often she needed a nurse. Robert was there for her on both counts. She managed to send the eldest son, Carter, to Harvard, because Harry had been so insistent on it. Smith, the next eldest, went to sea. Robert in his teens took over many of the household chores, from grocery shopping to money management. He took Ann out in the carriage, which—now that Harry was gone—she could afford, and lifted her spirits with foolery. Once, according to family tradition, she complained of feeling the air too much, so Robert playfully cut up some paper with his pocketknife to curtain the carriage for her.

He may have been her favorite, but she couldn't give him the same start in life that she had given Carter (who had lived high at Harvard until Ann, no pushover for anyone after Harry, took him to task in a stiff guilt-inducing letter). When Robert was eighteen, and well prepared by the Alexandria Academy in mathematics and the classics, there was no money for college or to set him up in farming or business. Nursing his mother had given him an interest in medicine, but that too was out of the question.

(At this time Abraham Lincoln, two years younger than Robert, was educating himself by the light of the fire and taking on odd jobs that would lead in time to frontier lawyering, but that was not a course open to a Virginia gentleman.)

There were family connections. With the backing of Secretary of War John C. Calhoun, Senator Andrew Jackson, and several congressmen, Robert in the spring of 1824 obtained an appointment to the U.S. Military Academy at West Point. Because there were so many applicants, he would have to wait a year to become a cadet, but now he had firm prospects. To get a leg up on advanced mathematics, he enrolled in a class taught in Alexandria by a man named Hallowell, who recalled many years later that Robert "was gentlemanly, unobtrusive, and respectful in all his deportment. . . . One of the branches of mathematics he studied with me was Conic Sections, in which some of the diagrams are very complicated. He drew the diagrams on a slate; and although he well knew that the one he was drawing would have to be removed to make room for another, he drew each one with as much accuracy and finish, lettering and all, as if it were to be engraved and printed."

In June of 1825 Robert left home to begin his education as a professional soldier. Many years later he would call this the greatest mistake of his life.

Ann hadn't wept when Harry left, but as soon as Robert was out the door she sobbed, "How can I live without Robert? He is son, daughter and everything to me!"

CHAPTER TWO

ROBERT WAS as meticulous in his spelling as in everything else he undertook. And yet in his two-sentence letter accepting the West Point appointment, which we would expect him to have read over several times (and which is the earliest letter in his handwriting known to exist), he wrote: "I hereby accept the appointment . . . with which I have been honnoured [*sic*]."

The *u* in that last word was at variance with Noah Webster's dictionary of 1806, which made a point of rejecting the British way of ending words in *-our* when *-or* would do, but *honour* is what you would expect from a conservative Southern cavalier of Norman-French lineage who had likely read the Rev. Aaron Bancroft's *Life of Washington,* in which *honor, ardor, favor,* and the like ended resoundingly in *-our.* In fact Lee stuck with *honour* (and *labour, valour, endeavour*) all through the Civil War, as we can see in those dispatches and letters of his that survive in his handwriting.

Despatches, he spells it, which was common enough at the time. Also *Traveller, devined,* always *agreable* rather than *agreeable;* and he lowercases *french, english,* and *yankee.* All traceable to Anglo-Francophone roots—or to the fact that his only formal modern-language study had been in French, not English. He Frenchified his mother's and his daughter's name—*Anne,* although they both spelled it without the *e.* "We have consumed three large pound cakes," he writes to his daughter Agnes during the war, "besides smaller choses." His *controul* seems less accountable—but that's the way Alexander Pope spelled it. *Decrepid?* John Dryden and Washington Irving spelled it that way. He hardly ever misspells anything else—and never again *honour* with an extra *n.*

It is as if, when the eighteen-year-old Robert hit the *h*-word, an imp of the perverse seized him. By no means was he ever disillusioned enough to write, as Ernest Hemingway did after World War I, that "abstract words such as glory, honor, courage or hallow were obscene," but he had reason to appreciate, at least subconsciously, that this particular word was heavily and precariously loaded.

In *Honor & Slavery,* Kenneth S. Greenberg argues that in order to justify owning slaves, antebellum Southern aristocrats placed an extraordinary and complex premium on honor. In making a great show of dignity and self-mastery, and portraying slaves as lacking all propensity for such qualities, they polarized themselves from the human beings they treated as property. In this connection, enormous significance was vested in the nose:

> For Southern men of honor, the nose was . . . the most prominent physical projection of a man's character, and it was always exposed to the gaze of others. Little wonder that men of honor should regard the nose as the most important

part of their bodies. As one antebellum Southern writer described it in a humorous, but also deadly serious, article on noses, "No organ of the body is so characteristic as the nose. A man may lose an eye or an ear without altering his features essentially. Not so with the nose." He went on to describe a man with "a most extravagantly protuberant nose"—a nose that "moved to and fro like a pendulum"—who had decided to have it trimmed by a doctor. "I saw him afterwards," he wrote, "and did not recognize him. I do not recognize him now, nor do I intend to. His individuality, his whole identity is lost. . . . The features do not fit; they become incongruous; he is himself no more; for, in truth, the individuality of a man is centered in his nose. Hence it is that nature, to indicate its great importance, has granted us but one nose, while all other organs are supplied in pairs." . . . Clearly, he was comparing the nose to the eyes and the ears. The liver, the heart, the penis, and the stomach were not even considered. A man's character was expressed in what could be publicly displayed. . . . One of the greatest insults for a man of honor, then, was to have his nose pulled or tweaked.

If there is one feature that stands out in portraits of every Lee, it is the nose. The Lee nose is if anything even more handsomely Roman than George Washington's. It is the antithesis of a slave's nose. Robert E. Lee's father had suffered his nose to be nearly severed, literally, and financially he had cut off his own.

By the time Robert was applying to West Point, Light-Horse Harry was not the only Lee who had dishonored his family.

Harry's first son by his first marriage, Robert's half brother Henry Lee IV, who had inherited Stratford from his mother (her father having taken care that it not go to Harry), was on his way to earning the sobriquet "Black-Horse Harry." He admitted adultery with his teenage sister-in-law and ward, Betsy, who bore a child that died—but not naturally, rumor had it—at birth. He had also entangled Betsy's fortune in legal encumbrances when she sued him for abuse of his guardianship, and he had let Stratford run down and allowed it to pass out of the family. (In time Betsy married respectably. She and her husband bought Stratford and fixed it up again.) The scandal would not become public until 1830, but by 1825 Robert knew that as far as the honor of the Lees was concerned, his work was cut out for him.

So he went through West Point without a single demerit. Never late, never insubordinate, ever impeccable in uniform. At Groton young Franklin Delano Roosevelt soon realized that his perfect deportment was making him unpopular among his peers, so he began acquiring a respectable number of "black marks" on purpose. This was not Robert E. Lee's way. "The Marble Model," his fellow cadets called him. He was named an assistant professor of mathematics and was awarded the highest rank in the corps: cadet adjutant. He finished second scholastically in the class of 1829. (George Mason, a New Yorker, who finished first, was also clever enough to resign his commission after one year and settle prosperously in Iowa.) Aside from one course taught by the chaplain, which covered geography, history, ethics, and law, his studies were in engineering, math, science, drawing, tactics, strategy, and French for the sake of exposure to French texts on engineering, math, tactics, and strategy. In his spare time he read a new edition (prepared by Black-Horse Harry) of Light-Horse Harry's memoirs, the works of Alexander Hamilton, a volume of Napoleon's memoirs in French, and, also in French, the *Confessions* of Jean-Jacques Rousseau, whose proposal "to show my fellows a man as nature made him, and this man shall be myself" we may presume Lee did not find congenial.

A fellow cadet recollected, after the war, that Robert's "personal appearance surpassed in manly beauty that of any cadet in the corps. Though firm in his position and perfectly erect, he had none of the stiffness so often assumed by men who affect to be very strict in their ideas of what is military. His limbs, beautiful and symmetrical, looked as though they had come from the turning lathe, his step was elastic as if he spurned the ground upon which he trod."

He made friends—lifelong ones in Jack Mackay of Georgia and Joseph E. Johnston, a Virginian whose father had fought for the United States with Light-Horse Harry and who would fight against them with Robert. Johnston would also recall that the young Robert "was the only one of all the men I have known that could laugh at the faults and follies of his friends in such a manner as to make them ashamed without touching their affection for him, and to confirm their respect and sense of his superiority."

If Robert participated in collegiate high jinks, it was with prudence. Jefferson Davis, an older fellow cadet, threw a forbidden drinking party and urged Lee to attend, but Lee said no, he had to study. Davis, who would be his Confederate commander in chief, accumulated debts to tailors and merchants. Lee's account book at the end of his schooling showed a positive balance of $103.58.

While he was away, his mother's health deteriorated. He spent his only furlough from the Point, two months in the summer of 1827, traveling with her and his brothers and sister Ann, who had married a Marshall, to socialize with landed relatives. (Carter, the only brother who would take a drink, was the witty cynosure, Robert being recalled as dignified and gracious.) Their mother by then had advanced tuberculosis. The next time Robert saw her, right after graduation, she was on her deathbed, in a relative's home. Since marrying Harry she had moved from one borrowed house or guest bedroom to another, depending upon the kindness of cousins.

Robert attended her in her last days. "When he left her room," writes Douglas Southall Freeman, "her gaze followed him, and she would look steadily at the door until he entered again."

CHAPTER THREE

ROBERT'S TWO SISTERS inherited from their mother her twenty-thousand-dollar trust fund, her personal effects, and a few house slaves. Robert and his two brothers, together, received a tract of land in southwestern Virginia, which was encumbered with back taxes and from which Robert was never to realize any income, and several more slaves. They probably sold some of the slaves. Common shabby-cavalier practice.

Robert specifically was bequeathed his mother's maid, Nancy, and her children. He rented them out—presumably, for he was kind, placing them all together with a tolerable master. His sister Mildred inherited Nat, the elderly like-a-member-of-the-family house servant and coachman, but Nat was apparently suffering from the same disease that had carried Ann away. On the assumption that a warmer climate would ease Nat's last days, Robert took him along to his first army posting: Cockspur Island, Georgia, where, according to a fond early biographer, he "nursed him with the tenderness of a son." And who is to say he didn't? If there was any master to whom slave management was filial duty, as we shall see, it was Marse Robert.

Cockspur Island, however, does not sound like the kind of place anyone would go to for his health. Robert was twenty-two. At that age his father had been a cavalry hero dashing about to create a new nation. Robert's performance at West Point had enabled him to choose a commission in the Corps of Engineers, which in 1829 was considered the elite of the army. But the mission of the Corps of Engineers, then and now, is far from romantic. Cockspur Island lies on the Savannah River below the city of Savannah. Brevet Lieutenant Lee (he had the rank of lieutenant, but not yet the full pay) was assigned to assist in laying the groundwork for the construction of a fort there, in a stretch of mud, in which he spent much of his time immersed to his armpits. He didn't complain.

His West Point friend Jack Mackay's family lived in Savannah. Robert fell in love with Jack's sisters, Margaret and Eliza, one after the other, rather as his father had done with Ann's cousin and then Ann. The Mackay girls would remain his affectionate friends throughout his life, but they preferred other suitors. Later, when Robert learned of Eliza's impending nuptials, he wrote to her, "[T]his cannot be Miss Eliza (my sweetheart). . . . I have been in tears ever since the thought of *losing* you." This was six months after his own marriage.

His bride was his childhood playmate Mary Anna Randolph Custis. She was the pampered, almost idolized only child (her siblings having all died in infancy) of the well-born Mary Lee Fitzhugh and the wealthy, slovenly dilettante

George Washington Parke Custis, who was himself the grandson of Martha Washington and the step-grandson and adopted son of the only man Light-Horse Harry looked up to: the dignified, self-controlled, honorable, and distant Virginian general of generals, George Washington.

Mary had a very Norman nose. Otherwise, in portraits that must have been meant to flatter, she looks dumpy and vague. She had, like her father, artistic leanings. So, in a small way, did Robert, but we have no evidence that he exchanged sketches with her as he did flirtatiously with other ladies. (The only extant drawings of his are rather nice side views of a turtle and an alligator, thoroughly inked in and given feisty stances and interestingly sentient, though not anthropomorphic, facial expressions.) Mary was one of the few women in Robert's life about whom he was not passionate, except insofar as worry can be a passion.

He relished dancing, gossip, parties; she had an aversion to all these. He admired stoic fortitude; she often complained. He was elegant; she was dowdy. He was the essence of discipline; she was slapdash and habitually tardy. He needed a mate flexible and hardy enough to move with him from post to often spartan post; she was a frail, spoiled homebody who longed always for the servants and rose gardens of Arlington.

Since Robert could scarcely support Mary in the style to which she was accustomed, her father at first opposed the marriage, but her father was not formidable. ("Washy," George Washington Custis had been called as a young man, or "Tub" because he was chubby.) Many years later Robert would condemn novels—"They paint beauty more charming than nature, and describe happiness that never exists." But he was reading to Mary and her mother from a new novel by Sir Walter Scott (whose "girly-girly" romanticism Mark Twain would blame, rather sweepingly, for the Civil War) one day, when the mother suggested that the young folks take a break for refreshments. Over fruitcake Robert proposed and Mary accepted.

The marriage made him George Washington's step-great-grandson-in-law. It connected him to a fortune and a great house, and also to a warm family circle in which he had felt secure and loved as a child. It was perhaps, given his own lack of a fortune or prospects of leisure, and the shadow of dishonor cast by Harry and Henry, the only socially suitable match available to him.

Here is how Lee described his wedding in a letter to his commanding officer back at Cockspur, who had been unable to attend:

> So, Captain, you would not come up to Arlington on that memorable Thursday.... However you would have seen nothing strange, for there was neither fainting nor fighting, nor anything uncommon which could be twisted into an adventure. The Parson had few words to say, although he dwelt upon them as if he had been reading my Death warrant.... I am told I looked "pale and interesting" which might have been the fact. But I felt "bold as a sheep" and was surprised at my want of Romance in so great a degree as not to feel more excited than at the Black Board at West Point.

The couple honeymooned at the estates of relatives, one of whom was moved to observe, "[M]y eye fell upon his face in perfect repose, and the thought at once flashed through my mind: 'You certainly look more like a great man than any one I have ever seen.'" In August 1831 the newlyweds were posted to Fort Monroe, Virginia, where they resided for two years in cramped junior officer's quarters. Mary brought along one of her slaves, Cassy, but she also commenced ordering "Mr. Lee" about as if he were a servant, which she would continue to do throughout their marriage. It was from Fort Monroe that Robert wrote Eliza Mackay of his dismay at her marrying another: "And how did you disport yourself, My Child? Did you go off well like a torpedo cracker on Christmas morning?" Perhaps it was different in the mid–nineteenth century, but toward the end of the twentieth a survey indicated that American wives regarded a husband's *emotional* involvement with other women as more disturbingly unfaithful than extramarital sex. There was, however, nothing surreptitious about Robert's romantic friendships. Mary, who would later write that "the society of the ladies . . . seemed the greatest recreation in his toilsome life," added a formal congratulatory note at the bottom of that letter to Eliza, mentioning in passing that "I am now a wanderer on the face of the earth."

Some sixty miles away from Fort Monroe, Nat Turner led by far the biggest insurrection in the history of American slavery. Sixty slaves killed fifty-five white people. The revolt was put down quickly, without Robert's involvement. He decried the hysteria that it spread among Virginia slave owners. He did express concern about the reaction of some ladies who were to be his houseguests—warning them in a letter that "Mrs. Lee is somewhat addicted to *laziness & forgetfulness* in her housekeeping." Mrs. Lee for her part wrote to a friend,

"[T]here are not many persons here very interesting." A little over a year after their wedding, she bore him their first child, George Washington Custis Lee, nicknamed Boo.

Mary returned to Arlington for several lengthy spells. Once Robert wrote to a male friend that upon her departure he was "happy as a clam at high water." To Mary he wrote, "Let me tell you Mrs. Lee, no later than today, did I escort Miss G. to see Miss Kate! . . . How I did strut-along." To Jack Mackay he wrote, "I would not be unmarried for all you could offer me," but also, "As for the Daughters of Eve in this country, they are formed in the very poetry of nature, and would make your lips water and fingers tingle." When he traveled himself to Arlington for a grand "frolick" celebrating his brother Smith's marriage, he wrote to his superior officer, Capt. Andrew Talcott, another male friend (whose merry wife, Harriet, he addressed as "my beautiful Talcott"), "My spirits were so buoyant when relieved from the eyes of my Dame, that [his new sister-in-law] was trying to pass me off as her spouse but I . . . deceived the young ladies and told them I was her younger brother. Sweet innocent young things, they concluded I was single and I have not had such soft looks and tender pressures of the hand for many years." He wrote to Harriet often, gushingly, over the years. Later he began a lifelong correspondence with his wife's younger cousin Martha Custis "Markie" Williams: "Oh Markie, Markie, when will you ripen?" And "Did you not feel your cheeks *pale* when I was so near you? You may feel pale; but I am happy to say you never write as if you were pale; and to my mind you always appear bright and rosy."

The army sent Robert the romantic to reinforce the foundation of Fort Calhoun, on a man-made rockpile island off the Virginia coast called Rip Raps, which was sinking. He responded dutifully, supervising the piling on of another layer of rocks. The Rip Raps kept sinking.

He was called to Washington to serve as assistant to the head of the Corps of Engineers. This enabled him to reside with Mary and their two-year-old boy at Arlington and commute across the Potomac. At this point Robert's mother-in-law proposed that he resign from the army and take over the affairs of Arlington, so that Mr. Custis could devote himself to aesthetic pursuits. Custis particularly enjoyed painting heroic portraits of George Washington—starting at Washington's feet and working upward. The effect (judging from one reproduction, in which Washington's feet look too small to support how the rest of him turned out) was odd. According to Robert's great-granddaughter Anne Carter Zimmer, "When one canvas was rejected from the Capitol rotunda, where artists showed their works, Custis directed his agent to throw the picture in the Potomac, 'that it may offend no more.' Later a visitor saw it being hauled out, the 'dim figures of men, & horses . . . to be boiled off & the canvas used for aprons,' for Mr. Custis was also chronically strapped for cash." He couldn't even afford a saddle horse.

Robert would often say that all he really wanted to be was a farmer. Arlington would be his family's home base, and he would wind up taking over much of the responsibility for keeping up Mr. Custis's neglected properties anyway. But he chose to stay in the army. No Virginia cavalier, even one who had been left unlanded, would work, even titularly, under a man who could afford to devote his time to epic poems but couldn't maintain a horse to ride.

Nor could any cavalier look up to President Andrew Jackson and the other vulgar Democrats who held sway in the capital in the 1830s. Jackson may have recommended young Robert to West Point, but he represented the sort of people who had mutilated Light-Horse Harry. To the extent that Robert deigned to take any interest in party politics he was a neo-Federalist, which made him more or less, by default, a Whig. His work in Washington entailed deadly boring official correspondence and some lobbying with Congress—which deepened his dislike of Democrats—in the interests of the Corps of Engineers' budget. He was happy to get away on a summer-long mission to resurvey the hotly disputed boundary between Ohio and Michigan. His wife, pregnant and ailing, implored him to return immediately. He responded, "[W]hy do you . . . tempt [me] in the strongest manner, to endeavour to get excused from the performance of a duty, imposed on me by my Profession, for the pure gratification of my private feelings?" He continued to plot a line across bits of wild country and Lake Erie. While he was gone his second child, Mary Custis Lee (to whom Robert would refer as "Daughter"), was born.

When he returned, official duty discharged, his wife had embarked upon a lifetime of illness. She was in bed suffering from a pelvic infection, abscesses of the groin. Doctors also diagnosed something along the lines of rheumatism. They cupped her and leeched her. Her hair got "in such a *snarl*," as Lee put it in a letter, that she "took the scissors and cut it all off." She got better, but then the babies came down with whooping cough—"whooping, coughing, teething, etc. and sometimes all three together," as Lee wrote to a friend. Then Mary got the mumps. He looked after her, but less cheerfully, it would appear, than he had attended his mother.

In peacetime, promotion came slow—finally a first lieutenancy in 1836, after seven years of active service. Lee felt he couldn't press for reassignment out of Washington because of Mary's condition. His little daughter caused him to write, "Oh, she is a rare one, and if only sweet sixteen, I would wish myself a cannibal that I might eat her up," but his prospects depressed him, and he felt obligations closing in. At the May 1837 birth of William Henry Fitzhugh Lee, whom his father nicknamed Rooney, he wrote, "I am the father of three children . . . so entwined about my heart that I feel them at every pulsation."

The Mississippi River gave him an out. The river was attempting, as it will, to change its course, in such a way as to leave the bustling river city of St. Louis stranded. Lee leaped at the chance to keep the Mississippi in its place, which necessitated leaving his dependents entwined about the in-laws. "I shall leave my family in the care of my eldest son," he wrote jocularly to Talcott. Little Custis was five, Robert's age when his father came home broken.

Not for a moment, in his heart, was he as absent as his father had been. "My Sweet little boy, what I would give to see him!" he had written Mary earlier after being separated from her and Custis. "I am waking all night to hear his sweet little voice, & if in the morning I could only feel his sweet little arms around my neck & his dear little heart fluttering against my breast . . ." And now, with regard to the two-year-old Rooney, "If I could only get a squeeze at the little fellow turning up his sweet mouth to 'keese Baba!'" If in those letters from Papa afar there is something of the obsessive and idealized quality of his effusive letters to other men's wives, there is also something almost childishly touching about them.

But Baba was also writing Mary in reference to one of the boys, "You must not let him run wild in my absence." His fourth child, Ann Carter Lee, known as Annie, was born while he was away. He was doing some fine riparian engineering, moving two thousand tons of rock, building well-placed dikes that saved the St. Louis harbor, and making heroic efforts to reduce expenses so as to stay within a niggardly budget. But politics, local and congressional, pulled the plug on his project. Four years on the Mississippi—for part of which he persuaded his family to join him—advanced his career not at all. His active, admirably selfless support of a former commander who had incurred the disfavor of the Jacksonians did not ingratiate him back in Washington, where he returned in January of 1841 to await reassignment, staying at Arlington again. Mary presented him, he wrote to a friend, with "*another* little Lee, whose approach, however long foreseen, I could have dispensed with for a year or two more. However, as she was in haste to greet her Pa'a [*sic*], I am now very glad to see her." This was Agnes, the fifth. The other children had "most obdurate colds, & opened upon this newcomer with such an incessant barking, that all my care and attention were required to keep them from her captivating presence."

When he was not being treated, himself, with twenty

leeches for the grippe, other captivating presences caught his eye. "You are right in my interest in pretty women," he wrote a male friend, "& it is strange that I do not lose it with age." He added, "Young men, however, ought not to lead them into indiscretions, & fighting duels or shooting each other can't remedy it."

He was next assigned to Fort Hamilton, in New York Harbor, where after a while the family joined him. A little terrier that he had saved from drowning gave birth to puppies, one of which the children kept, named Spec. After Spec jumped out of a second-story window to follow the family to church, he was allowed to sit with the family during Sunday services. This *may* provide some context for the only surviving evidence of Lee's capacity for outright hilarity, as follows.

One evening at Fort Hamilton, Lee happened to enter a junior officer's quarters as a heated argument was under way over Episcopal liturgy. In England the Oxford Movement was advocating that Church of England rituals and institutions be elevated to something more like those of Roman Catholicism. Priestly absolution, literal body-and-blood eucharist, more elaborate vestments, even nunneries and brotherhoods. Controversy over all this had reached the point of violence in England. "Puseyism," this movement was called by its opponents, after one of its leaders, a priest and Oxford don named Edward Bouverie Pusey.

Some of the young officers deplored the spread of Puseyism in the United States. Others were as staunchly in favor. Lee was amused. He stepped forward and advised Lt. Henry Hunt in a liturgical tone, "I am glad to see that you keep aloof from the dispute that is disturbing our little parish. . . .

But I must give you some advice about it, in order that we may understand each other. *Beware of Pussyism! Pussyism* is always bad, and may lead to unchristian feeling; therefore beware of *Pussyism!*" Hunt noted that the "ludicrous turn given by the pronunciation, and its aptness to the feeling that one or two had displayed, ended the matter in general bursts of laughter."

Whenever Lee met Hunt thereafter, Lee would look at him "in a grave way, shake his head, and say, 'Keep clear of this *Pussyism.*'" Lee's sense of humor is a study in itself. (See Appendix II.)

CHAPTER FOUR

IN THE 1840s the always frugal Lee got a bit more than sol-
vent by careful investment of his slave-rental income. If he
were to die, his wife and children—six of them, when Robert
junior came along in 1843—would not be left to their own de-
vices as Light-Horse Harry's had been. When the weather
precluded construction work in New York, he and his family
could winter at Arlington. But Custis's boarding school cost
three hundred dollars a year, nearly a fourth of a captain's
salary, which was sometimes reduced from one year to the
next by Congress. Robert went back and forth from Fort
Hamilton—he was there when the seventh child, Mildred,
was born at Arlington in 1846—to staff duty in Washington.
Both jobs were tedious.

Fortunately for his career, hostilities were brewing on the
border between Mexico and Texas. In 1836 Texas had won independence from Mexico, and in 1845 it accepted annexa-
tion by the United States as a slave state, but Mexico's
definition of Texas was considerably smaller than Texas's, and
it was willing to fight over the difference. The Polk administration decided that America's manifest destiny should in-

clude not only all of Texas but all of California above the
Baja and the New Mexico Territory (including what is now
Arizona) as well. America went to war. Freshman Congressman Abraham Lincoln of Illinois said the hostilities had
been started by "the sheerest deception." In Concord, Massachusetts, Henry David Thoreau went to jail overnight for refusing to pay a poll tax supporting the war—he saw it as a
scheme to extend slaveholding territory. Thoreau wrote an essay, "Civil Disobedience," advancing a principle of passive
resistance that would eventually influence the civil rights
movement in the United States. "When a sixth of the population of a nation which has undertaken to be the refuge of
liberty are slaves, and a whole country [Mexico] is unjustly
overrun and conquered by a foreign army, and subjected to
military law," Thoreau wrote, "I think it is not too soon for
honest men to rebel and revolutionize."

Lee had his own, Whiggish, reservations. "It is true that
we have bullied [Mexico], and for that I am ashamed," he
wrote (meaning by "we" Polk's Democrats). But he applied
with alacrity for combat duty, and wrote to nine-year-old
Rooney a letter containing a strange parable:

I do not think I ever told you of a fine boy I heard of [who]
lived in the mountains of New Hampshire. He was just thirteen years of age, the age of Custis. . . . The snow there this
winter was deeper than it has been for years, and one day he
accompanied his father to the woods to get some wood.
They went with their wood-sled, and, after cutting a load
and loading the sled, this little boy, whose name was Harry,
drove it home while his father cut another load. He had a

fine team of horses and returned very quickly, when he found his father lying prostrate on the frozen snow under a large limb of a tree ... which had caught him in its fall, and thrown him to the ground. He was cold and stiff, and little Harry, finding that he was not strong enough to relieve him from his position, seized his axe and cut off the limb and rolled it off of him. He then tried to raise him, but his father was dead and his feeble efforts were all in vain. Although he was out in the far woods by himself, and had never before seen a dead person, he was nothing daunted, but backed his sled close up to his father, and with great labor got the body on it, and, placing his head in his lap, drove home to his mother as fast as he could. The efforts of his mother to reanimate him were equally vain ... and the sorrowing neighbors came and dug him a grave under the cold snow, and laid him quietly to rest. His mother was greatly distressed at the loss of her husband, but she thanked God who had given her so good and brave a son. You and Custis must take great care of your kind mother and dear sisters when your father is dead. To do that you must learn to be good.

Not long before, Rooney had managed, while playing with a mechanical straw cutter, to sever two of his fingertips. Remarkably, they were successfully reattached by a surgeon— Lee sat up several nights with Rooney to make sure that the bandages stayed on while he slept. Rooney displayed soldierly sang-froid, but his unblemished father was horrified that the son who had inherited his looks might be "maimed for life." Lee wrote to Custis, away at boarding school, "If children could know the misery, the desolating sorrow with which their acts sometimes overwhelm their parents, they could not have the heart to thus cruelly afflict them. May you never know the misery I now suffer." And, "I hope this will be a lesson to him and that in time he will correct his evil ways." Rooney regained full use of his hand, and Lee expressed especial relief that "the disfiguration is less than I anticipated." The limb cutting in the parable may have derived somewhat from that experience. Not to mention Light-Horse Harry's nose.

But Emory Thomas has a point in suggesting that "Lee was this Harry. He was certainly not Light-Horse Harry. He encountered, even expected, frustration; but he . . . accepted his life and dealt with its vagaries in the most positive ways that he could. Lee was that nine-year-old in the woods with a frozen father."

In Mexico, under fire, the Light-Horse in Robert would thaw, temporarily.

In all his life Lee found three living male figures whom he loved and could rely upon for strength and support commensurate with his needs. Two of them, his great horse Traveller and his "right arm," Stonewall Jackson, he had yet to meet. The first of the three was his commander in Mexico, Gen. Winfield "Old Fuss and Feathers" Scott, a pomp-loving but hearty and effective warhorse, a hero of the War of 1812, a prominent Whig, the commanding general of the U.S. Army, six foot five and surpassingly stout. (Scott reviewed the cadets of West Point in 1839, when U.S. Grant was a plebe. "With his . . . quite colossal size and showy uniform," Grant would recall in his memoirs, "I thought him the finest specimen of manhood my eyes had ever beheld.")

Lee spent the last three months of 1846 making his way to northern Mexico, where he did a bit of engineering work, pontoons and so on, and also rode fifty and sixty miles a day on his horse Creole, reconnoitering. Once at night he thought he had found a hillside covered with enemy tents, but at dawn he saw that the tents were sheep. Then Scott, who had been impressed by Lee's potential in a previous encounter, summoned him to join the inner circle of his staff—his "little cabinet" of four advisers. On Lee's fortieth birthday, January 19, 1847, he set off on Creole, with his Irish servant, Jim Connally, to ride 250 miles to join the forces that were preparing to land near Vera Cruz, in the south, and advance eastward upon Mexico City.

He found time to write to Custis and Rooney: "I shall not feel my long separation from you if I find that my absence has been of no injury to you, and that you have both grown in goodness and knowledge, as well as stature. But, ah! how much I will suffer on my return if the reverse has occurred! You enter all my thoughts, into all my prayers; and on you, in part, will depend whether I will be happy or miserable, as you know how much I love you. You must do all in your power to save me pain." His family made him feel far more vulnerable than combat was about to.

Scott's force of eight thousand men landed unopposed, and prepared to besiege the walled city of Vera Cruz. Returning from a reconnaissance with Lt. P. G. T. Beauregard, Lee was shot at for the first time—by (not for the last time) an

American. Just behind friendly lines, a man stepped forward and cried, "Who goes there?" "Friends!" cried Lee, as Beauregard simultaneously (and perhaps characteristically) cried, "Officers!" Whether because these responses thus overlaid sounded, to this enlisted man, like Spanish, or like a contradiction in terms, or because this kind of thing often happens in war for no particular reason, the man—an undertrained volunteer who by various accounts was a picket, or was lost, or may have been a deserter, though where he can have hoped to desert to around there is hard to imagine—fired a pistol at Lee from twelve feet away. After Lee and Beauregard pounced on the man and took his pistol, Lee checked himself and saw that his uniform was singed. The bullet had passed between his body and his left arm. He didn't turn a hair.

Part of Lee's job was to direct the construction of gun emplacements. On the fifth day of heavy artillery fire back and forth ("My heart bled for the inhabitants," Lee wrote home. "The soldiers I did not care much for, but it was terrible to think of the women and children"), Vera Cruz surrendered. One of the naval officers who had joined in the cannoneering was Robert's big brother Smith Lee, whose arrival brought out Robert's protectiveness. "No matter where I turned," Robert wrote, "my eyes reverted to him, and I stood by his gun whenever I was not wanted elsewhere. Oh! I felt awfully, and am at a loss what I should have done had he been cut down before me. . . . He preserved his usual cheerfulness, and I could see his white teeth through all the smoke and din of the fire."

To show their goodwill, Scott, Lee, and other American

officers attended Catholic mass inside the conquered city. They were asked to join priests in a solemn procession, holding candles. This made Scott nervous, because anti-Catholic sentiment was high back in the States, and he feared that news of his participation would hurt his political future. (In point of fact, when he ran as the Whig Party candidate for president in 1848, the Catholic-hating Know-Nothings accused Scott of Catholic sympathies and abandoned the party, contributing to Scott's resounding defeat and the party's demise.) One of the other officers happened to be Lt. Henry Hunt, late of Fort Hamilton. He nudged Lee. "I really hope," he said, "there is no *Pussyism* in all this."

Lee tried not to smile.

As Scott's forces advanced inland from Vera Cruz, their way was blocked by the army of Antonio López de Santa Anna, who, after assuming the wartime presidency of Mexico, had put up stiff resistance to Gen. (and future President) Zachary Taylor in the north. Lee went out scouting on foot, surveyed the terrain adroitly, and concluded that the only feasible way to attack was through an all-but-impassable ravine. As he stopped at a spring, he heard Mexican conversation.

He dropped behind a log. And there he stayed all day, as Mexican soldiers drank from the spring, chatted, sat down on the log with their backs close enough to touch, moved on, and were replaced by others. One soldier stepped over the log, putting his foot down right next to Lee. Bugs crawled all over Lee and bit him as he lay frozen, breathing as quietly as possible. Finally night came, and the soldiers moved away toward campfires. Now he had to find his way back in the pitch dark.

And he did. And he went back the next day, with a detail that cut a path through the ravine. Thanks in large part to his work, Scott's army routed the Mexicans, so precipitately that Santa Anna left behind his carriage and his wooden leg. In his report on the battle, Scott wrote:

> I am impelled to make special mention of the services of Captain R. E. Lee, engineers. This officer, greatly distinguished in the siege of Vera Cruz, was again indefatigable . . . , in reconnaissances as daring as laborious, and of the greatest value. Nor was he less conspicuous in placing batteries, and in conducting columns to their stations under the heavy fire of the enemy.

To his son Custis, Robert wrote, "You have no idea what a horrible sight a battlefield is." His eye as ever drawn to poignant femininity, he told of a young Mexican girl who was trying to extricate a small boy, whose arm was shattered, from under a dying soldier.

> Her large black eyes were streaming with tears, her hands crossed over her breast; her hair in one long plait behind reached her waist, her shoulders and arms bare, and without stockings and shoes. Her plaintive tone of *"Mille gracias, Signor,"* as I had the dying man lifted off the boy and both carried to the hospital still lingers in my ear.

In two more victorious battles, Lee's exertions in reconnaissance—scrambling for miles back and forth over rough and unknown blocks and fissures of lava in the rain and dark—and in infantry advances under fire caused Scott to report that "the gallant, indefatigable Captain Lee" had performed "the greatest feat of physical and moral courage . . . by any individual in my knowledge."

Then, in early September, eight months after Lee had joined Scott, the army confronted a heavily defended Mexico City, where Lee exerted himself even more heroically. He scouted out approaches, reported to and conferred with Scott, checked artillery locations, guided troops to the base of the seemingly impregnable two-hundred-foot cliff called Chapultepec, looked after the stricken Gen. Gideon Pillow (whose wound proved as negligible as his name must have seemed apt), and finally joined Scott for his triumphant entry into the city after Chapultepec had been scaled and conquered. "Men," bellowed the lionhearted Scott, "I could take each one of you to my bosom." By this time Lee had been up and working, under pressure and in harm's way, for fifty-six straight hours. He was also bleeding from a slight unspecified wound. For once in his life, he fainted, right off his horse. Scott himself revived him, with a nip from the general's brandy flask. This may have been Lee's first taste of strong drink. In his trunk was a bottle of whiskey that a well-wishing Virginia lady had given him in case of just such an emergency. He returned to Arlington with it unopened.

Scott had taken six thousand men into uncharted terrain and humiliated a much larger army on its own ground. In the process, according to a confidant, he had taken "an almost idolatrous fancy" to Lee. In an official communication Scott called Lee "the very best soldier that I ever saw in the field."

The cosmopolites of Mexico City, feeling no particular attachment either to Santa Anna's regime or to Texas, New Mexico, and California, entertained Scott's army with fiestas. Lee befriended a little Franco-English girl, with blue eyes and long dark lashes, improbably named Charlottelita, and took her and her elder sister to see the art collection in the national palace. He did not gain any respect for the Mexican people, though. Exploring the countryside one day alone, he suspected that an old man he saw was about to lasso him. He drew his pistol, and the local man dropped his lariat.

One reason for Mexico's vincibility was civil strife between its various states, which could not cooperate in its defense. As a result of the war, what had been 40 percent of Mexico's territory became new grounds for disunion in the United States, throwing off the tenuous balance that had been achieved by hard-won political compromises between pro- and antislavery states. The ease with which the Mexican forces had been overwhelmed by old-fashioned into-the-breach tactics encouraged a complacency in American military thinking that would lead to senseless slaughter of Americans in the next war.

Mexico won Lee three brevet promotions, all the way up to colonel. He had proved himself to be as splendid a warrior as his father. And he had been embosomed at last by a father figure, a larger-than-life one at that. He would be tempted to give up soldiering over the next decade, but in what other line could he hope to feel such a rush of worthiness? Here in this disciplined, seat-of-the-pants adrenaline was ... pleasure. And he had proved to his satisfaction what his father would have approved: Though you may be outnumbered, never let yourself be trapped. Don't be defensive. Attack. Cleverly, but above all boldly.

The Mexican War, however, was not the American Revolution. It was a land-grab, and a big chunk of the land, Texas, became a slave state. Political enemies accused Scott of bribing his way to victory, and he was relieved of command. Lee did not find his promotions gratifying, because just as much advancement had come to so many other officers who had seen little action but had political connections. At any rate, Robert's swashbuckling days were over.

He'd been away from Arlington for twenty-one months. He returned on horseback. The little dog Spec ran to greet him, but the younger children hung back. They seemed, Lee wrote his brother Smith, "to devote themselves to staring at the furrows in my face and the white hairs in my beard." Hugs and kisses all around. "But where's my *little* boy?" Lee cried. "He then," Rob recalled years later, "took up in his arms and kissed—not me, his own child in his best frock with clean face and well-arranged curls—but my little playmate, Armistead! I remember nothing more of any circumstances connected with that time, save that I was shocked and humiliated." It would be his earliest memory of his father.

But Robert had imported for his namesake a Mexican pony, named Santa Anna, and had time now to give him riding lessons. At forty-one he was still spry enough to compete with his older sons in the high jump, when they set up a bar in the yard. He kissed and caressed the little ones, and they dutifully tickled his feet. He was away again on various assignments, but kept returning to an energetic and affectionate family circle. He tried to talk Custis out of military aspirations, but Custis was determined, and went to West Point. Liquor was found in his room. Placed under arrest, he denied all knowledge of how the jug got there, and wrote to his father forthrightly all about it. From the tone of his earlier preachments, you might think that Father would have come down hard, but he wrote back that Custis's letter had given him "more pleasure than any that I now recollect having ever received. It has assured me of the confidence you feel in my love & affection, & with what frankness & candour you open to me all your thoughts." Custis got off with eight demerits, and Robert wrote to him again sympathetically. (He seems to have been somewhat easier on Custis, who would never make much of a soldier, than on either of his other sons, who would.)

In 1852, though Robert would have preferred wider-ranging outdoor duty, he was assigned to West Point as its superintendent. In fact the duty suited him, and his family. Mrs. Lee was sickly, but she gardened and gamely gave parties. Robert fished and rode with the children whenever he could and kept a close eye on their development. A very close eye—when Rob returned from swimming lessons, "[m]y father inquired constantly how I was getting along, and made me describe exactly my method and stroke, explaining to me what he considered the best way to swim, and the reasons therefor."

He took an *in loco parentis* interest in every cadet. Oliver O. Howard, who would lead troops against Lee's in several major battles of the Civil War, was so intent as a youth upon saving the soul of everyone he met that he was shunned at the Point, by everyone except Lee, who was kind. (Lee also told Custis, who stood second in his class, behind Howard, "You must crowd that boy Howard. You must be No. 1." At graduation Custis was.) Then there was cadet James McNeill Whistler, whose mother resided not far away in Scarsdale, New York.

She fussed over her son. Lee once had to apply to the chief of engineers in Washington so that Whistler could get special permission to receive "some articles of underclothing" from her. When Mrs. Whistler wrote asking that Jimmy be granted a special leave to see her off for Europe, Lee's response was pained, but he acceded.

Whistler's father, George Washington Whistler, was a military man of distinction who, like Harry Lee, resigned his commission in a fit of pique. He died when James was still a boy. Maybe in Whistler—who had already developed a great facility in drawing—Lee saw a bit of himself. He managed to keep the lad enrolled for a while, in spite of demerits in the three figures, but Whistler's heart was not in the military. Once, when charged with being absent from parade, he retorted to his cadet superior, "If I was absent without your knowledge or permission, sir, how did you know I was absent?" Finally, when Whistler flunked yet another course, chemistry, by responding to his first exam question, with simple dignity, "I am required to discuss the subject of silicon. Silicon is a gas," Lee had no choice but to approve his dismissal, with what sounds like genuine regret. Whistler went to Paris, and began to come into his own as artist, eccentric, and maker of enemies. Years later, when Lee heard of his former cadet's success in the arts, he smiled and said, "Little Jimmy Whistler!" With a different allocation of energies, Lee himself might have cut a broad swath in Paris. (Assuming he would not have been, in Paris, a bit like the stalwart American in Henry James's *The Ambassadors,* Lambert Strether, who says: "To be right. . . . That, you see, is my only logic. Not, out of the whole affair, to have got anything for myself." To which the worldly Miss Gostrey replies, "It's not so much your *being* 'right'—it's your horrible sharp eye for what makes you so.") As it happened Whistler, born in Lowell, Massachusetts, decided at West Point that he was a Southerner, and he remained one abroad. One of his several ways of irritating Europeans was proclaiming his firm support for slavery.

The higher-performance West Pointers, including the even-then-dashing J. E. B. Stuart, came by the superintendent's house wanting to get a look at daughter Mary, who was seventeen. They came away saying that their superintendent, up close, was the handsomest man they ever saw.

Once when Lee and son Rob were out riding, Rob recalled, "We came suddenly upon three cadets far beyond the limits. They immediately leaped over a low wall . . . and disappeared from our view. We rode on for a minute in silence; then my father said: Did you know those young men? But no; if you did, don't say so. I wish boys would do what is right; it would be so much easier for all parties!"

That is the kind of disciplinarian that Lee would be as a commanding general. Forbearing toward others, hard on himself. The cold weather at West Point, he wrote to a lady, "is as harsh to me as my duties & neither brings any pleasure."

...

In 1855 his situation changed, but not for the better. Winfield Scott, who was still the army's top general, was telling people that "if I were on my death-bed tomorrow, and the President of the United States should tell me that a great battle was to be fought for the liberty or slavery of the country, and asked my judgment as to the ability of a commander, I would say with my dying breath, 'Let it be *Robert E. Lee.*'" But being Scott's boy was of limited advantage to a man who lacked all capacity for assertive self-promotion.

Settlers out west needed protection from Indians. Colonel Lee was transferred from the engineers to the cavalry. Secretary of War Jefferson Davis said that "the son of Light-Horse Harry Lee now seemed to be in his proper element." But the job was no plum. Lee took charge of two squadrons of the Second Cavalry at Camp Cooper, in Texas, roughly in the vicinity of what is now Abilene and then, by a long shot, wasn't even that. He lived in a tent, he rode the plains. Whereas his father had taken to Indians, had ridden into battle beside them, Lee found them repellent. He met Chief Catumseh of the Comanches and his six wives, and wrote home: "Their paint and ornaments make them more hideous than nature made them and the whole race is extremely uninteresting."

He looked everywhere for a cat to adopt but couldn't find one in that rough country, so he fretted over the chickens he kept, which seemed to take a shine to him:

> This morning I found an egg at my tent door, & a few minutes since another hen seems desirous of presenting me with

another. After walking around my chair & peering up at my writing, she hopped upon my bed, but disliking such intimacy I rose to dislodge her when she skimmed across my table, upsetting my ink.

He built the hens a "house of twigs," which furnished "little protection against rain. Soldier hens, however must learn not to mind rain." He also kept a pet rattlesnake and fed it frogs.

In the summer of 1856 he led a punitive expedition against a hostile Comanche chief, across sixteen hundred miles of West Texas wilderness, "the most barren and least inviting country I have ever seen." The chief and his marauders got away.

As usual, Lee was anxious about his children's behavior. Rooney, having tearfully accepted his father's insistence that he was not West Point material, had gone to Harvard. He never wrote. (Of how many great generals can it be said that they wrote to their children more often than their children wrote to them?) Rooney's boyish unruliness evoked in his father an almost panicky severity. Lee was sent around Texas to serve on court-martials of men who had got into tedious trouble through just such lapses as he was afraid Rooney was tending toward. Lee worried that Rooney thought "entirely of his pleasures." Rooney's fellow student at Harvard, Henry Adams, would describe him in *The Education of Henry Adams* as a natural leader of men, and a blockhead.

Back home Mrs. Lee was more and more hampered by what seems to have been rheumatoid arthritis, and then she bounced a check, making Robert nervous for the family reputation. Some loud children being ignored by their mother set Lee bizarrely off on the subject of "infant intercourse & infant business, when each child brings its stock of selfish animalism, to aggravate that of its playmates," underlining "the necessity & advantage of *self-denial & self-controul.*"

Back east, lesser men with connections were promoted ahead of him. He was depressed. But a rare letter from "the old Roon" cheered him up. A "big two-fisted fellow with an appetite that does honor to his big mouth," Robert said of Rooney, who didn't have his father's looks. What inspired Robert to give William Henry Fitzhugh Lee the nickname that stuck with him all his life? Unlike his older brother Custis, Rooney never had his father's finely chiseled features. His face was fuller, rounder, more like his mother's. Did Rooney, in the cradle, strike his father as looking Irish, therefore infra-Cavalier? Or did he look as if he would become (as he did) the bluff, hearty fellow his father was too conflicted to be? At any rate Rooney, class of '58, had had enough of Harvard by 1857. He still wanted to be a soldier, like his father. Winfield Scott arranged for him to be commissioned as a second lieutenant, infantry.

To one of his daughters Lee wrote blithely from Texas. He had seen a cat with "two holes bored in each ear, & in each were two bows of pink & blue ribbon. His round face set in pink & blue, looked like a big owl in a full blooming ivy bush." In admonition he is wooden and apprehensive. In appreciation of ribbons, pretty faces, flowers, he comes alive. Children, he wrote in a diary around this time, "should be governed by *love* not *fear.*"

Easier said than lived up to consistently. Like another principle of governance—that all men are created equal. In

1857 the U.S. Supreme Court in *Dred Scott* v. *Sandford* held that a slave was property, with no rights as a citizen even outside of slave territory, and that the Congress could not prohibit slavery in unsettled territories. Decades of legislative compromise between slave states and free states were undone, and antislavery forces were infuriated. In that same year Lee's father-in-law died and left him a bad case of what Rudyard Kipling, decades later, would call "white man's burden."

CHAPTER FIVE

MARY LEE WAS her father's sole survivor, and she was a woman. She inherited the use of Arlington during her lifetime, but the title went to her eldest son, Custis. In not naming his son-in-law as principal heir, Mr. Custis may have had in mind the profligacy of Light-Horse and Black-Horse Harry Lee. But it was he himself who had been fiscally irresponsible. He left debts of more than ten thousand dollars and virtually no cash, and there were sizable liens on the estate's other plantations, White House and Romancoke. Lee was named executor. He would have to sort out thousands of encumbered acres and 196 slaves. All those people, the will directed, were to be emancipated within five years.

During the postbellum century, when Americans North and South decided to embrace R. E. Lee as a national as well as a Southern hero, he was generally described as antislavery. This assumption rests not on any public position he took but on a passage in an 1856 letter to his wife. The passage begins: "In this enlightened age, there are few I believe, but what will acknowledge, that slavery as an institution, is a moral & political evil in any Country. It is useless to expatiate on its disadvantages." That may sound a bit like people who would describe smoking (in a climate of opinion different from the more censorious one toward that addiction than obtains today) as "a filthy habit," while making no great effort to quit smoking themselves.

He goes on in this letter,

I think it however a greater evil to the white than to the black race, & while my feelings are strongly enlisted in behalf of the latter, my sympathies are more strong for the former. The blacks are immeasurably better off here than in Africa, morally, socially & physically. The painful discipline they are undergoing, is necessary for their instruction as a race, & I hope will prepare & lead them to better things. How long their subjugation may be necessary is known & ordered by a wise Merciful Providence. While we see the Course of the final abolition of human Slavery is onward, & we give it all the aid of our prayers & all justified means in our power, we must leave the progress as well as the result in his hands who sees the end; who Chooses to work by slow influences; & with whom two thousand years are but as a Single day.

In 1848, just before he departed for the Mexican War, Lee had written out his will, which was never superseded. The only slaves it mentioned were the ones he had inherited from his mother nineteen years before: "Nancy & her children . . . all of whom I wish liberated so soon as it can be done to their advantage and that of others." Given the last four words, that gesture rings hollow. As long as their manumission was not to the advantage of "others," they would be stuck. Lee's position was that slavery was God's will, and the only people who had any discretion in allowing God's will to evolve were slave owners. It must be said, however, that although Nancy's children by that time must have been adults, Lee had kept that little family together and, loosely speaking, in his: at White House.

"Although the Abolitionist must know this," he continued in his 1856 letter,

> & must See that he has neither the right or power of operating except by moral means & suasion, & if he means well to the slave, he must not Create angry feelings in the Master; that although he may not approve the mode by which it pleases Providence to accomplish its purposes, the result will nevertheless be the same; that the reasons he gives for interference in which he has no Concern, holds good for every kind of interference with our neighbors when we disapprove their Conduct. . . . Is it not strange that the descendants of those pilgrim fathers who Crossed the Atlantic to preserve their own freedom of opinion, have always proved themselves intolerant of the Spiritual liberty of others?

Those "others" would be the people on whom he believed the yoke of slavery to rest more heavily than it did on the slaves themselves. With regard to slavery Lee was no freethinker. (See Appendix III.)

Though it was hardly "strange" that anyone outside the South should be unable to see how the material liberation of slaves could impinge on the "Spiritual liberty" of planters, Lee had a point about the self-righteousness of New Englanders, many of whose racial judgments were abstract and condescending. And even while pressing for immediate abolition, Northerners sometimes agreed implicitly with Lee's concern that emancipation was no miracle cure. During the war, after having come into contact with rescued slaves in his role as a Union officer, Henry Adams's brother, Charles Francis, concluded that slavery had rendered Southern blacks "as supine as logs or animals," not because it was harsh but because it encouraged shiftlessness. The slave, he said during the war, "is the foot-ball of passion and accident, and the fit of freedom may prove his destruction." After the war Charles would be so impressed with Lee's character as to suggest that a statue be erected in his honor.

Before the war, however, slavery had done to Lee, at least intellectually, what debt and the mob in Baltimore had done to his father: backed him into a dishonorable corner. In order to defend, in effect, a system that he instinctively deplored because it put him in the camp of oppression, Lee wrapped his class in a grotesquely ill-fitting banner of offended civil liberty and Christianity. And how much weight does a political statement have, when you express it only in a letter to your wife? If we found a letter from Richard Nixon to Pat in which he declares that war is evil, would we call him antiwar? In fact Lee's letter to Mary has a tinge of passive aggression: It was Mary's domestic needs and her family's holdings that had involved him in this evil.

His father-in-law's will made him a land-poor planter, drastically underfunded and required to liberate his labor force within five years. Arlington had been allowed to run down—fallen fences, leaking roof, overgrown lawns, slaves who for years had been compelled to do little work aside from cultivating their own vegetable gardens. He couldn't sell it because Mary and the children needed it, and it was designated the children's inheritance. With the support of Winfield Scott, who was still commanding general of the army, Robert obtained leave so that he could see to the property.

By this time both of his adult sons, Custis and Rooney, were army officers. Rooney wanted to marry his distant cousin Charlotte Wickham, and the White House plantation seemed ideal for them to start a life in, but he couldn't leave the army at this point because he was on his way to Utah. (The federal government had declared Brigham Young's Mormons to be in "a state of substantial rebellion.") Custis was on duty in San Francisco, but he might have resigned his commission and become a planter. The will had made him titular inheritor, after all. He had something of Robert's noble countenance and also his melancholic tendency. Of all the Lee boys he seems the most father-directed. But Lee seemed to go out of his way to discourage Custis from stepping into the breach. "No place is without its drawbacks," Lee wrote to him, as if Custis proposed to come home in order to escape the hard army life, "and you must not expect unalloyed pleasure anywhere."

Custis then offered to transfer his inheritance to Robert. Though he wrote back that he was "impressed by your filial feeling of love and consideration," Robert declined, and assumed the onus without the entitlement. Some months later, he wrote to Rooney, "I am . . . trying to get a little work and to mend up some things. I succeed very badly." He had to nurse his wife, by then badly crippled, and two of his daughters, who were also in bad health. "I feel that I ought to be with my regiment," he wrote, "and this feeling deprives me of half the pleasure I derive from being here."

He had no enthusiasm for slave driving. The emancipation of the Custis chattel had to be approved in the courts, and this proceeded slowly. "Scarcely had my father been laid in his tomb," Mary Lee wrote to an acquaintance, "when two men were constantly lurking about here tampering with the servants & telling them they had a right to their freedom *immediately* & that if they would unite and *demand* it they would obtain it. The merciful hand of a kind providence & their own inertness I suppose prevented an outbreak." When Lee hired out some of the Arlington slaves to other plantations, three of them, he wrote, "returned the first day on account of the work being too hard. Among them is Reuben, a great rogue & rascal whom I must get rid of some way."

That was not the end of it. "I have had some trouble with some of the people," he wrote to Rooney. "Reuben, Parks, Edward . . . rebelled against my authority—refused to obey my orders, & said they were as free as I was etc. etc. I succeeded in capturing them however, tied them & lodged them in jail. They resisted till overpowered & called upon the other people to rescue them." He sent them to an agent who hired them out elsewhere. (Five years later, in the midst of the war, he would write to Mary, "I am sorry to hear of Reuben's death.") Later at least two Arlington slaves escaped and got as far as Maryland before being captured. They too were hired out.

North of Virginia, abolitionist sentiment was running high, and the Custis heritage was prominent enough to attract controversialist attention. In June 1859 two anonymous letters written from Washington appeared in Horace Greeley's outspokenly antislavery *New-York Tribune*. They alleged that Lee was overworking and underfeeding his people and declared, "Last week three of the slaves ran away; an officer . . . overtook them nine miles this side of Pennsylvania, and brought them back. Col. Lee ordered them whipped. They were two men and one woman. The officer whipped the two men, and said he would not whip the woman, and Col. Lee stripped her and whipped her himself." These were followed by a third anonymous letter denouncing the first two as provocateurs' lies, which they palpably were.

Harry Lee would have leaped at such bait, but Robert, anything but polemic, made no public response. After reading the letters, he wrote to son Custis that father-in-law Custis "has left me an unpleasant legacy." Virginia gentlemen had complained for generations that slavery in general was an unpleasant legacy. How unpleasant, they would begin to learn in two years.

At Rooney's wedding, Robert shone. The bride, Charlotte, was lovely and had already become one of her father-in-law's many favorite women ("Chass," he called her), but a guest called Robert "decidedly the most striking person in the room."

His wheat harvest in 1859 was, he wrote, "a great failure." And yet after two years the farms were in better shape, and the father-in-law's debts, except to Robert, had been paid off. Rooney, having acquitted himself well against the Mormons, had taken up residence with his new wife at White House, and Custis had been assigned to the War Department in Washington, to which he could commute from Arlington. One morning in October 1859 Robert was preparing to return to his regiment in Texas at last when one of his favorite old West Point cadets, 1st Lt. J. E. B. Stuart, arrived with a message for him: He was to proceed to Harpers Ferry, Virginia, on the Potomac River on the Maryland border, to deal with what appeared to be a slave revolt.

"Servile rebellion" was the term often used at the time. We can't begin to understand what drove the slave states to recoil violently from the Union unless we get a sense of the fascination and dread loaded into this oxymoronic term. From early in the history of the Republic, slave states enrolled great percentages of their able-bodied white men in untrained and ill-regulated militias, largely out of insurrection phobia. (The vexed question of the American citizenry's untrammeled right to bear arms may derive from this concern.) Slaves had no rights, and yet they were deemed indispensable to the region's economy. They prepared the ruling class's food, introduced okra into it, could just as well introduce poison. They made their masters' beds, which many of the masters found disappointingly unmusky compared with the slaves' own pallets at night. Favored house slaves were said to be like members of the family, but that didn't mean the family felt right about according them surnames or allowing them to have legal families of their own. When they accepted Jesus as their lord and savior, they seemed to enjoy him more than white folks did. They clapped on the offbeat. Their masters could not regard them as entirely human, for then how could their oppression be justified? And yet lifelong, grotesquely asymmetrical bonds of affection developed. (The former slave owner Thomas Chaplin, however, after looking over his antebellum plantation diary, came to the postbellum conclusion that "the Negroes did not care as much about us as we did for them.") Intimacy and order mingled with otherness and wrong.

And puritans and transcendentalists of the North presumed to cast simple religious judgment from afar? Northern Republicans railed against "slave power" as an arrogant force threatening to enslave the whole country. The white South felt—*was*—enslaved by slavery. It was a grossly inefficient system, and it could not be reformed. But abolition of it, Jefferson Davis opined, would lead to the extinction of the black race, because ex-slaves would not be able to provide themselves with the necessities of life.

The South's wealth, not to mention a good deal of the North's, was bound up in slavery. Divestiture would be nearly as disruptive to the economy as abolition of the stock market would be today. Beyond that, slave owners had a messy moral interest in preserving the culture they had inherited. They feared the unknowns involved in whatever intermediate steps might be made toward emancipation. If ex-slaves proved unequal to the challenges of freedom, the transition would be chaos. If they proved readily equal to it, slave owners would be convicted retroactively as tyrants. Subjective grounds for denouncing both the feckless dependency of slaves and the abolition of slavery offered something like, we might say, the anxious/fervid moral languor enjoyed by those who wax indignant in this century against both homosexual promiscuity (the "lifestyle") and gay marriage.

Meanwhile, from a distance, New Englanders could live down the sins of their forefathers—witch trials had been easier to give up. The resultant moral, cultural, and practical morass bred lurid apprehension: Southern whites expressed a fear that if the slaves ever did rise up in numbers, the men of the South would be unable to fight back at first because their priority would be to shelter their wives and daughters from an unspeakable fate.

This could be justification for dealing unspeakably with anyone black and rising. One of the raiders at Harpers Ferry was a freedman named Dangerfield Newby, who hoped to free his still-enslaved wife and children, and hadn't raised enough capital to buy them. "Oh, Dear Dangerfield," his wife had written him, "come this fall without fail, money or no money I want to see you so much: that is one bright hope I have before me." When Newby saw that the insurrection could not succeed he tried to slip away into the town. He was shot in the head, his genitals and ears were cut off, sticks were jammed into his wounds, and he was thrown into the gutter, where free-range hogs tossed and worried and ate his remains.

Into this noxiousness Lee and Stuart strode crisply. They reported to President James Buchanan, who dispatched them to Harpers Ferry with one company of marines and four of Maryland militia. They arrived at Harpers Ferry that night. Lee, still in civilian clothes, quickly took charge.

"On arriving here on the night of the 17th," he later reported, "I learned that a party of insurgents, about 11 P.M. on the 16th, had seized the watchmen stationed at the armory, arsenal, rifle factory and bridge across the Potomac. . . . They had despatched six men . . . to arrest the principal citizens of the neighborhood and incite the negroes to join in the insurrection." But local slaves had not risen up. (The insurgents had entered the town on a Sunday night. When a Mr. Byrne was taken at gunpoint in the early hours of Monday and told, "We want your slaves," he had said, "You will have to do as I do when I want them—look for them. They went off Saturday evening and they haven't gotten back yet.")

The significant rising had been of armed citizenry, many of them drunk, and of both Virginia and Maryland militiamen. A reduced band of liberationists had barricaded themselves with thirteen hostages, black and white, in the fire-engine house within the armory enclosure. There they were trapped, like Light-Horse Harry in the Baltimore jail. A crowd surrounded the engine house, shooting at it sporadically. The raiders fired back through loopholes. A Quaker boy among them, who had promised his mother that he would not draw blood, had brought about the raid's sole measure of short-range emancipation by shooting the mild old mayor of Harpers Ferry, whose will, as it happened, directed that the small family he owned be freed at his death. The leader of the insurgents was rumored to be an old white man named Isaac Smith.

Lee took stock of the messy situation quickly and laid plans during the night. Out of courtesy, he offered the commander of the Maryland militia the honor of leading the attack. The amateur declined: "These men of mine have wives and children at home. I will not expose them to such risks. You are paid for doing this kind of work." He removed his hat and bowed when Lee took him off the hook. The Virginia militia commander followed suit. Lee turned to Lt. Isaac

Green, who commanded a party of marines sent by the War Department. "Lieutenant Green," he said, "would you wish the honor of taking those men out?" Green doffed his hat and accepted with thanks.

Early the next morning Lee sent Stuart, under a white flag, to the door of the engine house with a message requiring unconditional surrender. The message referred in the third person to both the sender of the message and the people to whom it was sent: "Colonel Lee represents to them, in all frankness, that it is impossible for them to escape." If the demand was rejected, as Lee suspected it would be, Stuart was to give a signal, and the marines would storm the place immediately, before the insurrectionists had a chance to bargain by threatening the hostages.

Stuart knocked on the door. It opened a crack. Stuart's china blue eyes took in the barrel of a carbine and the burning eyes of "Osawatomie" (he had started an abolitionist colony on the Osawatomie River in Kansas), John Brown. Stuart had seen this face before, while in Kansas with troops trying to police bloody conflict between proslavery and free-state guerrillas. In that territory Brown had led a party that took five proslavery men from their homes and hacked them to death with double-edged swords. With support from prominent abolitionists, Brown had stockpiled hundreds of firearms and pikes—spears, essentially—across the border in Maryland. He had tried to get Frederick Douglass to join him. After escaping slavery Douglass had taken his last name from a character in Sir Walter Scott's *The Lady of the Lake,* but he was not romantic enough to believe that this sort of revolt could succeed. He tried to talk Brown out of it. Undeterred, Brown had come into Harpers Ferry with five black men and thirteen whites in the evangelical conviction that he could seize the armory, rally an army of slaves, hide out in the Blue Ridge Mountains, and sweep through the Shenandoah Valley and on to the south, cleansing the nation of the institution he identified with Satan.

Brown tried to bargain with Stuart. Some of the hostages loudly endorsed the notion of further negotiations, but one was heard to shout, "Never mind us, fire!" Lee recognized the voice of Lewis W. Washington, grandnephew of George. "The old revolutionary blood does tell," Lee said quietly. Stuart stepped aside and waved his hat.

Some of the marines attacked the door with sledgehammers as others stood ready to charge in. Their rifles were not loaded. Lee had directed them to attack only with bayonets, lest they shoot a hostage accidentally, and the blacks inside were not to be injured unless they offered resistance, it being unclear whether they were conspirators.

Shots issued from inside the building. Lee, still in civilian clothes, stood exposed within easy range, but by one account Brown said, "Don't shoot him, he is unarmed." The sledgehammers didn't work, because Brown had tied the doors with rope inside, so that they would sag and rebound. But an improvised battering ram opened a small jagged hole in one door. Lieutenant Green forced his way into the dark station. "There is Osawatomie," said Washington. Brown was reloading his carbine. Green attacked him with his flimsy dress sword, gashing the old man's neck, trying and failing to run him through, and then whacking him down with the hilt. A marine's bayonet skewered one of the raiders and pinned him to the wall.

Three minutes after Stuart's signal, the firehouse was taken. Two marines had been shot, one fatally. Of Brown's seven remaining men, four, including one of his sons, were dead, and one, another of his sons, was dying. This son, gutshot in the night, had begged for hours to be put out of his misery, but his father said, "If you must die, die like a man."

"The dignified, gentle Colonel Lee, whose business was just this one of shedding blood," wrote Robert Penn Warren many years later, "gave the captives such consideration as he could." The wild, awful John Brown, whose business was just this one of freeing slaves, lay bleeding but composed.

All the hostages were safe. Washington refused to come out until he was provided with a pair of kid gloves, because he didn't want townsfolk to see how dirty his hands were. Then he adjourned to an inn with friends for breakfast.

Colonel Lee had accomplished his mission. If the rash old man who had been cornered and slashed and beaten down, and had led his sons to their death, stirred in Lee any recollection of his own father, he made no recorded mention of it. He was evidently not impressed—as Melville, Thoreau, Emerson, and Longfellow were, from afar—by an abolitionist's carrying his interpretation of the will of God to the point of martyrdom. After the capture Brown was interviewed at great length by a number of men, including Virginia governor Henry Wise, who called him "a bundle of the best nerves I ever saw cut and thrust and bleeding and in bonds." Stuart demanded of Brown, "But don't you read the Bible?" Lee questioned Brown only briefly, to get the names of his party. "The result proves that the plan was the attempt of a fanatic or a madman, which could only end in failure," Lee reported.

Fanatic or madman, well, yes. But this was *John Brown*. Long white beard of an Old Testament prophet, visage of a specter, ruthlessness of a pirate, serenity, in the end, of a saint. And Lee, by all accounts, thought the episode's significant figure was Lewis W. Washington. Seeing no more reason for general alarm than he had after Nat Turner's rebellion, Lee went home. But not everyone agreed with his "result proves" and his "could only end." Rumors abounded of rescue plots and imminent insurrection. Lee was ordered to return to Harpers Ferry with a security force. Brown's eloquent if disingenuous self-defense at his trial aroused, in the North, great sympathy for him and hatred of slavery, and in the South, paranoia. As Brown rode to the gallows, seated on his coffin, he took a good look at the Blue Ridge for the first time and said, "This is a beautiful country."

The hanging went off smoothly. Among the witnesses were Maj. Thomas Jackson, in command of cadets from the Virginia Military Institute, and John Wilkes Booth, who assured himself of a good view by passing as a Virginia militiaman. Jackson, who would go down in history as Stonewall and was nearly as extreme in his religion as Brown, wrote to his wife that Brown

behaved with unflinching firmness. . . . He stood on the trap door, which was supported . . . by a rope. . . . The rope was cut by a single blow, & Brown fell through about 25 inches, so as to bring his knees on a level with the position occupied by his feet before the rope was cut. With the fall his arms below the elbow flew up, hands clenched, & his arms gradually fell by spasmodic motions. . . . I was much impressed by the thought that before me stood a man, in the full vigor of health, who must in a few minutes be in eternity. I sent up a petition that he might be saved. Awful was the thought that he might in a few minutes receive the sentence "Depart ye wicked into everlasting fire."

The fiercely antiabolitionist Booth, who would take inflammatory action himself six years later, said, "Brown was a brave old man . . . a man inspired . . . the greatest character of this century." Brown suited enthusiasts on both sides: He confirmed abolitionists in their outrage and slave owners in their angry insecurity. Lee, the professional, had done his duty well, but Brown, the terrorist, had captured imaginations. He had done much to make inevitable the war Lee would fight.

CHAPTER SIX

EARLY IN 1860 Lee left Arlington again, to assume command of the military Department of Texas, in San Antonio. He wrote home that it was better for everyone that he be away from home. "I know I was very much in the way of everybody and my tastes and pursuits did not coincide with the rest of the household." He led an expedition that chased a bandit named Juan Cortinas into Mexico and lost him. After a lifetime of perfect health Lee was troubled by rheumatism and other pains that may have been the first signs of heart trouble.

In the fall of 1860 Abraham Lincoln was elected president. Lincoln's first priority was preserving the Union, but the "fire-eaters," as Southern hotheads were called, saw him as a cryptoabolitionist. After his election South Carolina seceded from the Union, and other Southern states followed. "As far as I can judge from the papers," Lee wrote his wife, "we are between a State of anarchy & Civil war. . . . It has been evident for years that the country was doomed to run the full length of democracy." No good thing, in a cavalier's eyes.

Texas, where he was stationed, became the seventh state to secede. "If Virginia stands by the old Union," Lee told a friend, "so will I. But if she secedes (though I do not believe in secession as a constitutional right, nor that there is sufficient cause for revolution), then I will follow my native State with my sword, and, if need be, with my life." He was ordered to leave Texas and to report in person to Gen. Winfield Scott in Washington.

No one knows what Scott and Lee, fellow Virginians, talked about. Scott was still the U.S. military's commanding officer, but at seventy-five and in failing health, he would be retiring within the year. Did Lee have with his mentor the sort of father-son chat he never had with Light-Horse Harry? Did Scott suggest that Lee was his natural successor? We know they both felt that war was the worst thing that could happen.

Scott had advised Lincoln to "let the wayward sisters go in peace," and insisted that the North at any rate was far from being prepared for war. He had yielded, however, to Lincoln's determination that federal property in the South be protected. Fort Sumter, in the harbor of Charleston, South Carolina, was held by a small Federal force. Lincoln had tried to be conciliatory, but rather than evacuate these troops he decided to dispatch supplies to Sumter by ship. Confederate cannons stopped the shipment. Jefferson Davis had long opposed secession, but he had stood with his state, Mississippi, and had been elected president of the Confederate States of America. He ordered Gen. P. G. T. Beauregard of Louisiana, who had been removed from his post as superintendent of West Point for his secessionist views, to fire on Fort Sumter, whose garrison soon surrendered.

The North took secession as an act of aggression, to be

countered accordingly. Lincoln called on the loyal states for troops to invade the South. "We are engaged in a war in which they will conquer us, or we shall conquer them," said *Harper's Weekly.* "They are coming to the Lakes, or we are going to the Gulf. The victory on one side or the other will be radical and final. It will be a social as well as a military victory. It will be like the Normans in England."

The fear of "servile rebellion" was replaced in the South by a resolve to pursue another oxymoron that should have been even more frightening: "civil war." Southerners preferred to call it the War Between the States. After all, the United States were regarded North and South as a plural: "The United States themselves," wrote Walt Whitman in 1855, in the first edition of *Leaves of Grass,* "are the greatest poem." (The United States did not become, grammatically, an *itself* that *is* until after the war.) When Lincoln called on the loyal states for troops to invade the South, Southerners could see the issue as defense not of slavery but of homeland. A Virginia convention that had voted 2 to 1 against secession, now voted 2 to 1 in favor.

Light-Horse Harry Lee would have been in the thick of the secession debate, or itching to get into it. Robert, at Arlington, left politics to the newspapers and the politicians. He was offered a Confederate brigadier generalship but apparently did not respond. Lincoln had promoted him from brevet colonel to full colonel. This he accepted. But when, after another chat with Scott, he was offered command of the field army Lincoln was raising to suppress secession, he declined, and when he read the news that Virginia had joined the Confederacy, he said to his wife, "Well, Mary, the question is settled," and resigned the U.S. Army commission he had held for thirty-two years. He probably had no faith that the Confederacy would prevail, but he wrote to his sister, Ann Marshall of Baltimore, who was a Unionist, and to his brother Smith Lee in Washington, "With all my devotion to the Union . . . I have not been able to make up my mind to raise my hand against my relatives, my children, my home." The governor of Virginia called him to Richmond and offered him command of "the military and naval forces of Virginia," with the rank of major general. He accepted. His people had been Virginians long before they were Americans.

Lincoln could never understand how such a fine man could fight for slavery; many army officers from deeper in the South stayed with the Union. But Arlington, Lee's home front, was right there on the cusp, where the fighting would be joined. Furthermore Lee's honor tied him not to a backwoods lawyer's sense of negotiational democracy but to the aristocratic tradition of George Washington and other honorbound Virginians like Patrick ("Give me liberty or give me death!") Henry, who had been quick to feel tyrannized by the British. Robert's generation of Virginians had been loath to desert the Union, whose founders had been their near forefathers, but now they were on their mettle. Slave owning may have stiffened that mettle. To the master submission is no abstraction.

Slave-state rhetoric was also highly mindful of *defilement*. John Janney, president of the Virginia convention that at last voted to secede, swung from sensibly opposing his state's secession to vowing "that no spot of her soil shall be polluted by the foot of an invader." Meaning by "her" Virginia, named for the Virgin Queen. The persistence of slavery in the United States offended abolitionists' sense of purity. Being regarded as impure got under the white South's skin.

Lee left Arlington again, to set about pulling together an army. Had he stuck with the Union, Arlington would not have been seized—"foully polluted," as he would put it in a letter to one of his daughters—by Union troops, as it soon was. It might have been seized by seceding Virginians. And Mary might have stayed with it. The war in Virginia might have begun right there, with Mary sitting adamantly on the front porch under fire, as she did in a borrowed house four years later while Richmond fell. As it was, she resisted Lee's repeated entreaties to evacuate. She wrote to Winfield Scott, asking him to allow her to stay. When that appeal was fruitless, she wrote to Mildred:

> Except to relieve your father . . . I would prefer not to stir from this house even if the whole Northern army were to surround us. The zealous patriots who are making their lines to *preserve* the Union founded by Washington might come & take the granddaughter of his wife from her home & desecrate it, for whatever I have thought & even *now* think, of the commencement of this horrible conflict, now our duty is *plain,* to resist unto death.

Observes Emory Thomas, "Had Lee chosen to remain in the United States Army or had he resigned and only raised corn while other men fought and died, he would have elected infamy. He would have had to spend the rest of his life explaining his actions to deaf ears. And not the least of a legion of accusers would have been his own wife, who became a fiercely partisan Confederate. Robert Lee would have been most in danger in his own bed. In a real sense, Lee went to war in order to avoid conflict."

Another of Lee's biographers, Margaret Sanborn, puts it this way: "He ignored the dictates of logic and reason and heeded the elemental call of Virginia." A damsel, a mother state, in distress. And maybe his father's shameful example had convinced him of this: The most hurtful and calamitous thing you can do is to look beyond the people you are closest to. Of this too, though: Don't get trapped.

Lee had an aversion to mass gatherings, to strangers generally. It was not in him to stand before a crowd and wax stentorian. After the war he would sit through an evening of oratory by his students at Washington College: many florid tributes to him, insults to the Yankees, and allusions to the beauty of Lexington's young ladies. His response would be, "You young men speak too long and you make three other mistakes. What you say about me is distasteful to me, and what you say about the North tends to promote ill feeling, and your compliments to the ladies would be more appreciated if paid in private." The only thing approaching a public address that he ever made was his speech to the Virginia convention, accepting command of its military forces, such as they were, as follows:

Mr. President and Gentlemen of the Convention: Profoundly impressed with the solemnity of the occasion, for which I must say I was not prepared, I accept the position assigned me by your partiality. I would have much preferred had your choice fallen on an abler man. Trusting in Almighty God, an approving conscience, and the aid of my fellow-citizens, I devote myself to the service of my native State, in whose behalf alone will I ever again draw my sword.

"Draw my sword" was a figure of speech, for he never carried a weapon in the Civil War, except for the ceremonial sword he borrowed for his surrender. His modesty as to his abilities, however, was not entirely rhetorical. As a staff officer, a reconnoiterer, a builder of dams and forts, he had certainly proved himself. But his field command experience had been limited to fruitless expeditions against Comanches and bandits. His only combat command had been against John Brown. Even on a personal level, he abhorred confrontation. But then, so did Ulysses S. Grant.

Lee was fifty-four and full of reservations, but he hit the ground running. He began with 18,400 names of amateur soldiers, militiamen of the sort who had declined to lead the assault at Harpers Ferry. Within a few weeks he had mobilized forty thousand troops, organized them into units stationed at strategic defensive points, and begun their training. His sons Custis and Rooney and his brother Smith exchanged their U.S. commissions for Confederate ones.

The women of the family, uprooted from Arlington by Federal troops, moved to various other estates deeper in Virginia. To daughter Mildred ("Precious Life"), Lee wrote in lightsome speculation about how the family cat was doing. "I saw a beautiful yellow cat . . . that reminded me of Tom. The latter no doubt lords it in a high manner over the British [that is to say, the imperialist foreigners, the Yankees] at Arlington. He will have strange things to tell when you next see him." Mrs. Lee was not to be jollied. She wrote her husband outraged letters. He urged her to summon Christian resignation and to retreat farther south. She was having none of that. She wrote in anger to the occupiers of her home, demanding that they at least restore to her those of her slaves as she found essential. The Yankees complied meekly. "I sympathize deeply in your feelings at leaving your dear home," Lee wrote her. "I fear we have not been grateful enough for the happiness there within our reach, & our heavenly father has found it necessary to deprive us of what He had given us." That can hardly have brightened her day.

Nor did other Southerners appreciate Lee's thoughts on what the war would bring. According to his aide Walter H. Taylor, Lee "looked upon the vaporific declamations of those on each side who proposed to wipe their adversaries from the face of the earth in ninety days as bombastic and foolish." Prominent men appealed to Jefferson Davis to assume military command, on the grounds that Lee was "too despondent." Davis decreed that every state's troops be incorporated into one Confederate army. Lee was back in a familiar role, as Davis's staff adviser.

So he didn't take part in the first real battle of the war, July 21, 1861, at Manassas, Virginia. Bull Run, the Yankees called it. (Northerners, being more urban, generally named a battle for natural features, while Southerners, being more pastoral and therefore taking mountains and streams for granted—or, conceivably, feeling too fond of them to associate them with carnage—generally named a battle for the nearest village or railroad station.)

At Manassas the Rebel yell was heard for the first time. Bell Wiley describes it in *The Life of Johnny Reb* as "an unpremeditated, unrestrained and utterly informal 'hollering.' It had in it a mixture of fright, pent-up nervousness, exultation, hatred and a pinch of pure deviltry." Gen. Jubal Early later compared it, favorably, to "the studied hurrahs of the Yankees." One wonders what Lee thought of it. He did not hear it in this battle, at any rate. Gen. Joseph E. Johnston and Gen. Pierre Gustave Toutant Beauregard of Louisiana commanded, Davis observed, and Lee—who had sent troops to Manassas and inspected them there—was left back in Richmond. "I wished to partake in the struggle," he told his wife, "and am mortified at my absence."

The Yankees were routed. It was the kind of fighting that the individualistic Rebs were best at, a mishmash of skirmishes and hand-to-hand collisions in which regimental organization went by the board. When one Confederate company commander turned to thank his charges at the end of the triumphant day, he found, according to a newspaper account, that the troops who had taken the last hill behind him had been "three of his own men, two 'Tiger Rifles,' a Washington artilleryman, three dismounted cavalry of the 'Legion,' a doctor, a quartermaster's clerk, and the Rev. Chaplain!"

Richmond celebrated and felt secure. Mary Chesnut was taking the air with lady friends one afternoon when, as she told her diary:

A man riding a beautiful horse joined us. He sat his horse gracefully, and he was so distinguished at all points that I very much regretted not catching the name as Mrs. Stanard gave it to us. He, however, heard ours and bowed as gracefully as he rode, and the few remarks he made to each of us showed he knew all about us. . . .

Perfection—no fault to be found if you hunted for one. As he left us, I said, "Who is it?" eagerly.

"You do not know! Why, it is Robert E. Lee, son of Light Horse Harry Lee, the first man in Virginia"—raising her voice as she enumerated his glories.

"All the same," Chesnut noted, "I like Smith Lee better, and I like his looks, too." (In at least one portrait, Robert's older brother Smith bears a remarkable resemblance to Cary Grant.) "I know Smith Lee well. Can anybody say they know his brother? I doubt it. He looks so cold and quiet and grand."

The South thought it knew that the war was won. Lee knew better. In the mountainous western part of Virginia, where Union sympathies were high (in 1863 it would become Federal West Virginia), Yankees under Gen. George B. McClellan held the upper hand over an ill-coordinated lot of Confederate commands. In July 1861 Davis sent Lee there to sort things out.

He failed. His authority was unclear, and he was not quite a great enough conciliator to mediate effectively between two former Virginia governors and bitter political rivals, John B. Floyd and Henry A. Wise. Though neither had a military background, they had been made brigadier generals by Davis and had recruited their own untrained troops. A third force was commanded by William Wing Loring, who was a professional but also a glory hound. Lee, a full general, outranked them all, but he was never one to *pull* rank, and even if he had been, he could hardly have unified these three, who resisted taking orders even from Davis. Cold rain fell steadily, nearly every day, turning such roads as there were to deep mud, and he wrote to Mary, "The measles are prevalent throughout the whole army."

He told her of riding to his new, miserable assignment over a stretch of road that he had last passed over in 1840, "on my return to St. Louis, after bringing you home. If any one had then told me that the next time I travelled that road would have been on my present errand, I should have supposed him insane. . . . The valleys so beautiful, the scenery so peaceful. What a glorious world Almighty God has given us. How thankless and ungrateful we are, & how we labour to mar His gifts." He was bucked up some by the presence of Rooney, now a cavalry major, "as sanguine, cheerful & hearty as ever. I sent him some cornmeal this morning & he sent me some butter."

He was accompanied to the Kanawha Valley by two of the slaves from Arlington, Perry and Meredith (whom he took care to supply with some of the cotton socks Mary sent for the troops), but whereas his father had dined in the field from silver plate, Lee made a point—as he would throughout the war—of eating and drinking from tin. Some nights on reconnaissance, at fifty-four not so hale anymore, he slept out in the cold rain in his buttoned-up overcoat. And there was no derring-do for him in this theater. In September he planned out what would have been a bold stroke against a Federal garrison at Cheat Mountain, but Loring got cold feet at the sight of the enemy and pulled back his troops. A month before, Lee had written to Mary, "Send word to Miss Sue W[ashington] that her father is sitting on his blanket sewing the strap on his haversac. I think she ought to be here to do it." That father, Lee's chief aide, John A. Washington, was reconnoitering with Rooney at Cheat Mountain when they ran into an ambush. Washington was killed. Rooney's horse was shot from under him. Rooney leaped onto Washington's horse and escaped under heavy fire: like grandfather, like father when younger, like son.

Lee finally cozened the Confederates into some measure of coordination, and tried to tempt the Yankees into attacking, but they wouldn't. When he returned to Richmond toward the end of October, most of western Virginia was still controlled by the Union. And Edward A. Pollard of the *Richmond Examiner* was one of several newspapermen who blamed Lee. Pollard called Lee "a general who had never fought a battle, who had a pious horror of guerrillas [Wise's irregulars], and whose extreme tenderness of blood induced him to depend exclusively upon the resources of strategy, to essay the achievement of victories without the cost of life."

On Lee's return he saw to it that Floyd, Wise, and Loring were transferred out of Virginia. But he had acquired the sobriquet, in the Richmond papers, of "Granny Lee."

The press printed rumors that the Lees' marriage was breaking up. Not true, but before Robert could visit Mary he was sent off on what he called, in a letter to Mildred, "another forlorn hope expedition." The coasts of South Carolina, Georgia, and northern Florida were vulnerable to invasion. Lee was sent south to organize the area's defenses. His reputation had sunk so low that Davis had to write to the governors of Georgia and South Carolina to inform them "what manner of man" he had sent. Lee's bearing, handsomeness, and lack of pretension won those gentlemen over. Many observers high and low were struck by such features as his "fine justly-proportioned head posed in unconscious dignity." He saved a baby—leaving his own baggage behind—from a fire that swept Charleston. He visited his father's grave on Cumberland Island for a few moments, was struck by the beauty of the roses near it, plucked a flower, came away, and did not share his thoughts with the aide who accompanied him. He wrote to daughter Mildred that he had "grown so old & become so changed that you would not know me. But I love you as much as ever, and you know how great a love that is." He acquired a fine gray stallion he named Traveller.

He also dealt with a host of logistical details and got grumbling troops started digging and constructing improvised earthworks that kept Savannah, for instance, from falling to the Yankees until 1864. But Port Royal, South Carolina, and Fort Pulaski, Georgia (whose foundation Lee had laid in the deep mud thirty years before), fell. News of disastrous Confederate defeats in Tennessee and North Carolina arrived. Lee summed up ten months of work in a letter to daughter Annie: "I have been doing all I can with our small means and slow workmen to defend the cities and coast here. Against ordinary numbers we are pretty strong, but against the hosts our enemies seem able to bring everywhere, there is no calculating. But if our men will stand to their work, we shall give them trouble and damage them yet."

In March 1862 Davis recalled him urgently to Richmond. Davis could not get along with either of his top generals in the field, Johnston and Beauregard, both of whom were highly competent. Nor could he get along with the Confederate Congress, which was not. He persisted in considering himself the commander in chief of all Confederate forces, which were woefully inadequate and falling back all around the South. Davis had hoped that by withholding cotton from European markets he could induce foreign powers to intervene on the side of the Confederacy, but that was not happening: The Union's naval blockade was preventing the importation of munitions. Johnston was pulling back from Manassas—which was beginning to look as if it might have been the high-water mark of the Confederacy—toward Richmond. General McClellan's army of one hundred thousand troops was preparing—slowly, since the North was wary of another Manassas, but inexorably—to attack the Confederate capital from one of several possible directions. Another force, of forty-five thousand Yankees, was nearby. Johnston's troops in northern Virginia numbered perhaps seventy thousand, and their year-old enlistments were ending. Davis's response was more pro forma than an effective delegation of command: He officially put Lee in charge of "the conduct of military operations in the armies of the Confederacy"—but "with duty at the seat of Government, under the direction of the President." For Lee this amounted to endless consultation and expanded paperwork.

He did manage to visit Mary at Rooney's estate, White House. She couldn't get around much, but she was knitting socks for soldiers at a furious pace. Custis was in Richmond, on Davis's staff, but Robert wasn't able to spend much time with him. Nineteen-year-old Robert E. Lee Jr., who Robert senior had hoped would remain at the University of Virginia, finally obtained his consent to enlist. The two went together to make sure that Rob was issued the blankets and gear he needed. "He got all his things and said he had all he wanted," Robert wrote to Mary. "I think he ought to have had another pair of pants."

Lee urged the habitually tardy Mary to move well south of White House, which was "too exposed to attack for the residence of a person as hard to move as you are. You would be captured while you were waiting 'a moment.'" At length she moved only a few miles away, to a neighbor's home, and in fact found herself behind the advancing Union line. General McClellan saw to it that she was returned to secessionist territory politely.

Meanwhile Lee was repressing his own feelings and ambition as he shuttled back and forth, like a child in a broken home, to mediate between the rigid, insecure egos of Davis (who had sent Beauregard out west) and Johnston. He sent diplomatic messages to his old friend Johnston almost pleading with him to communicate his intentions to Davis, who wanted to be in the field commanding the troops himself. Lee kept his own counsel. He was developing his own coherent notion of what could be done.

Johnston still had not made his intentions clear by May 31, when Lee and Davis rode—separately—to find out what was going on and found to their surprise that Johnston was in the process of attacking an isolated element of McClellan's force in the Battle of Seven Pines (Fair Oaks). The clash was inconclusive. There were five thousand Federal casualties and six thousand Southern, one of whom was Johnston himself. Lee and Davis saw him carried from the field on a litter. At last Davis freed Lee from staff duty, putting him in command of Johnston's army.

With that began, inauspiciously, Lee's apotheosis. For the first time he became a true battle commander, and we must try to assess his greatness in terms not just of character but of tactics and strategy. It is a presumptuous abstraction, however, to regard war as a general's medium.

From the troops' perspective, whatever honor may have been involved in the war was far outweighed by the squalor. When you read Bell Wiley's *The Life of Johnny Reb* and Sam R. Watkins's wonderful private's-eye view of the war in *"Company Aytch" or, A Side Show of the Big Show,* these things are tangible:

• Feet. Among the Confederate troops, a dearth of shoes. Men marched sixty miles barefoot on frigid mornings. When they could, they stitched together their own footwear. Wiley quotes a soldier's complaint that his rawhide sandals "stretch out at the heel . . . they whip me nearly to death they flop up and down they stink very bad and I have to keep a bush in my hand to keep the flies off them."

• The bad rations. "The beef is so poor it is Sticky and Blue; . . . if a quarter was thrown against the wall it would stick." Parched corn. Or green corn. Some days, nothing. Watkins writes that when he and his mates learned that the army besieged at Vicksburg was subsisting on rats, they weren't appalled; they were inspired to go hunting rats themselves. But when "I got a piece of cold corn dodger, laid my piece of the rat on it, eat a little piece of bread, and raised the piece of rat to my mouth . . . I had lost my appetite for dead rat." The food caused diarrhea that killed more soldiers than bullets did.

• The wounds. Watkins: "Some with their entrails torn out and still hanging to them and piled up on the ground beside them, and they still alive. Some with their under jaw torn off, and hanging by a fragment of skin to their checks, with their tongues lolling from their mouth, and they trying to talk. . . . In fact, you might . . . find men shot from the crown of the head to the tip of the toe. And then to see all those dead, wounded and dying horses, their heads and tails drooping, and they seeming to be so intelligent as if they comprehended everything."

• The horrible medical conditions. "Confederate surgeons," writes Wiley, "believed that suppuration, or 'laudable pus,' was an essential feature with the healing process. They probed with ungloved fingers; they deterred recovery by tampering with wounds; they worked in soiled uniforms; they used bloodstained bandages; and they were only partially conscious of the importance of clean instruments. It is not surprising in view of these and other shortcomings that gangrene played havoc with their patients." Bullets were probed for and limbs amputated without anesthesia. Untreated wounded were evacuated on wagons without springs over rocky dirt roads, their wounds rasped by fabric hardened by dried blood, as they cried, "Stop! Oh! For God's sake, stop just for one minute; take me out and leave me to die on the roadside." Concludes Wiley:

> Indeed no phase of Confederate history is so dark and tragic as that which reveals the incomprehensible torture endured by the sick and wounded. And if glory be measured by suffering, the South's greatest heroes are not those who died at the cannons' mouth at Cemetery Ridge . . . but rather those who, sorely wounded or desperately ill, lived to experience the unspeakable agony of hospitalization.

But then, should glory be measured by suffering? How about being in the right? The high moral ground, however, is a slippery slope—beware the commander who frets about holding it. If anybody's moral ground during the war was unimpeachable it was the slaves', and they presumably would have preferred something more to their benefit. If Lee was a glory hound, he was an extremely subtle one. He may, deep down inside, have gloried in his own suffering.

· The toughness of the veterans, their inurement to pain. Robert Stiles, in *Four Years Under Marse Robert,* tells of a man who, shot in the temple, got up, walked under his own steam to the hospital area, refused chloroform, and

> directed the surgeons in exploring the track of the ball, which had crushed up his temple and the under half of the socket of his eye, and lodged somewhere in behind his nose.

After they had extracted the ball and a great deal of crushed bone, he declared there was something else in his head which must come out. The surgeons told him it was more crushed bone which would come away of itself after awhile; but he insisted it was something that did not belong there, and that they must take it away immediately. They remonstrated, but he would not be satisfied, and finally they probed further and drew out a piece of his hat brim, cut just the width of the ball and jammed like a wad into his head; after that he was much easier.

• The extraordinary balm provided by the figure of Lee. "One evening," recalls Watkins,

General Robert E. Lee came to our camp. He . . . looked like some good boy's grandpa. I felt like going up to him and saying good evening, Uncle Bob! . . . I remember going up mighty close and sitting there and listening to his conversation with the officers of our regiment. He had a calm and collected air about him, his voice was kind and tender, and his eye was as gentle as a dove's. . . . I fell in love with the old gentleman and felt like going home with him . . . and when I saw that he was getting ready to start I ran and caught his horse and led him up to him. He took the reins of the bridle in his hand and said, "thank you, my son," rode off, and my heart went with him.

This was early in the war, before Watkins had seen the horrors of it, and he was recollecting in 1882, by which time Lee was established in the popular mind as a paragon. But many men wrote home that they continued to fight through the darkest hours only because Lee continued to lead them.

"I really believe," wrote Stiles, who had been an officer in Lee's army, "it would have strained and blurred our strongest and clearest conceptions of the distinction between right and wrong to have entertained, even for a moment, the thought that he had ever acted from any other than the purest and loftiest motive. I never but once heard of such a suggestion, and then it so transported the hearers that military subordination was forgotten and the colonel who heard it rushed with drawn sword against the major-general who made it." But then, consider this further effusion by Stiles:

I am not informed whether the figure of speech to which I am about to refer ever obtained outside the South. . . . It undoubtedly originated with our negroes, being an expression of their affectionate reverence for their masters, by metaphor, transferred to the one great "Lord and Master" of us all; but it is certainly also true that Southern white men, and especially Southern soldiers, were in the habit—and that without the least consciousness of irreverence—of referring to the Divine Being as "Old Marster," in connection especially with our inability to comprehend his inscrutable providences and our duty to bow to His irreversible decrees. There is no way in which I can illustrate more vividly the almost worship with which Lee's soldiers regarded him than by saying that I once overheard a conversation beside a camp fire between two Calvinists in Confederate rags and tatters, shreds and patches, in which one simply and sincerely inquired of his fellow, who had just spoken of "Old Master," whether he referred to "the one up at headquarters or the One up yonder."

While rich planters' sons were able to buy their way out of service, and overseers were exempted (one for every twenty slaves on a plantation) so that slaves couldn't escape and become "contraband," the war turned yeomen farmers—what Jefferson thought America should be a nation of—into virtual slaves. The great majority of the Confederate troops did not own slaves themselves (though they may have wanted some, and did have an investment in feeling superior to the ones they didn't have), so their motivation can hardly have been the defense of that institution as such. Taking them as the congeries of individuals reserving the inalienable right to straggle that they were, they were fighting to repel invaders, and they were sustained by cussedness, pride, loyalty toward their fellows, and antagonism toward men who were burning their homes and trying to kill them. To some extent they felt patriotic toward their new nation, at first. And they liked to fight. They were good at it. They didn't want to get whipped.

But for most of the war the Rebel troops fought because they were compelled to. After the Confederate Congress passed a conscription act that bound common men for the duration, "a soldier was merely a machine," writes Sam Watkins. "All our pride and valor was gone, and we were sick of war and the Southern Confederacy. . . . The boys . . . were shorn of the locks of their glory. They had but one ambition now, and that was to get out of the army in some way or the other." Only death or drastic disablement got them out, unless they managed, as many did, to escape. If after deserting they were caught, they were shot. If they returned after ten days' absence without leave (at least if they served under Gen.

Braxton Bragg) they were stripped naked, their heads were shaved, they were branded on each hip, and they were flogged, thirty-nine bloody strokes with a three-tailed rawhide whip. And then they were paraded through the ranks to the tune of "The Rogue's March." When Bragg was replaced by Gen. Joe Johnston, Watkins responded like a slave whose cruel master has been replaced by a just one. Johnston improved his men's food and clothes, and "[w]hen a man was to be shot, he was shot for the crimes he had done, and not to intimidate and cow the living, and he had ten times as many shot as Bragg had. . . . Instead of the whipping post, he instituted the pillory." But even those Johnny Rebs who weren't punished or wounded endured agony. Their working conditions were if anything worse than slaves'.

And Marse Robert—himself a professed unquestioning servant of God's will—was, as we have seen, a bad slave driver. Foreign observers were appalled by the lack of discipline in his army, between battles. His aide Walter Taylor complained that stragglers "wandered about the country like locusts, and were only less destructive to their own people than the enemy." The enslavement of those who did keep on fighting was sweetened by the extraordinary seemliness of their commander, but they were generally fed and outfitted more meagerly than Confederates in outfits deeper south. "Lee's Miserables," the soldiers of the Army of Northern Virginia began calling themselves as the war went on (a translation of *Les Misérables* was published in Richmond in 1863; copies were read in the trenches, the title got around by more or less phonetic word of mouth, and the pun took hold), and many of them seem, like Lee, to have prided themselves on their ability to tolerate their lot. They were as tough as, but also scarcely freer than, mules.

The men called the tough salted beef they sometimes gnawed on "mule meat." A common expression in the Confederate ranks—noted in the *Random House Historical Dictionary of American Slang* as a catchphrase, but not defined—was "Here is your mule!" Foot soldiers shouted it at mounted officers (though never presumably at Lee) who rode by, and they hurled it at the enemy as they shot at him. It must have meant something along the lines of "Kiss my ass." Men were made to inform on errant comrades by being threatened with "riding Morgan's mule," which meant being mounted on a sharp-edged timber set up ten or twelve feet off the ground. Sometimes heavy blocks, humorously called "spurs," were tied to the sufferer's feet. Morgan's mule (named, as was Mildred Lee's pet squirrel, Custis Morgan, for John Hunt Morgan, the daring cavalry commander who led a raid into Northern territory that captured Federal mules) tortured the crotch. And here is an anecdote from *"Company Aytch"*—the book Mark Twain might have written if he had stayed in, and survived, the war:

> One fellow, a courier, who had had his horse killed, got on a mule he had captured, and in the last charge, before the final and fatal halt was made, just charged right ahead by his lone self, and the soldiers said, "Just look at that brave man, charging right in the jaws of death." He began to seesaw the mule and grit his teeth, and finally yelled out, "It ain't me, boys, it's this blarsted old mule. Whoa! Whoa!"

The war was like that mule, and Morgan's. Hard to see any glory in it. It certainly didn't do the South any good. It did result in the freedom, de jure, of the slaves.

If men with Lee's capacity to embosom conflict instead of projecting it had controlled politics in 1861, there wouldn't have been a war. Like most leading Southern antisecessionists, Lee was a Whig. Whigs were what in the 1990s would be called triangulators: They kept trying to hold together a coalition of moderate Northerners and Southerners, who generally had in common nothing but opposition to Jacksonian democracy. The death of the Whig Party in 1852 divided the country into antislavery Republicans (including the former Whig, Lincoln) and proslavery or at least antiabolitionist Democrats. (There was no party, then, for Robert E. Lee.) Probably the United States could no longer bear slavery, and it took a cataclysm to wrench that institution out of the system. At any rate, in June 1862 the mule of cataclysm had taken the bit in its teeth. And Lee had other capacities.

You may recall Mr. Byrne, the slave owner who was one of John Brown's captives, the one whose slaves hadn't come back yet from Saturday night. As Brown's men were haranguing Byrne in his parlor, a female cousin of Byrne's walked in. "Cowhide those scoundrels out of the house," she demanded of him. "Why do you suffer them to talk to you?" Well, because they had him at gunpoint. Lee had something of that lady's reckless spunk. Combined with George Washington's poise. When he took over Johnston's command and renamed it the Army of Northern Virginia, McClellan's greatly superior force was gradually, cautiously, pushing it back toward Richmond. Lee resolved not just to cowhide

McClellan away from the Confederate parlor but to knock out his army and end the war before the South could be ground down. First he set his troops to digging and improving defensive positions between McClellan and Richmond. Those who had been calling him Granny Lee now called him the King of Spades. But Lee was getting ready to spur the mule.

CHAPTER SEVEN

You can read exhaustive arguments proving that Lee was a military genius worn down by the enemy's greater resources. You can read arguments just as exhaustive proving that he bungled the war. The consensus in recent years seems to have swung toward Grant's postbellum assessment (in which one of Lee's top lieutenants, Gen. James Longstreet, concurred): that Lee was a great defensive general but on offense he got away with murder, so to speak, until he didn't anymore. To be sure, some commanders were braver and more diligent than others, but every battle was largely subject to chance.

Communications and transportation were always iffy. Sometimes people showed up on time in the right place with the right armaments, and sometimes they didn't; and sometimes when they didn't they were more successful than when they did. A great deal of the time they were sick and exhausted. Sometimes providential hailstones fell. Nearly every battle that Lee was involved in came down to thousands of Blues or Grays charging a fixed position over a long stretch of open ground through a "tempest of iron and lead," in the words of Shelby Foote.

The great military historian John Keegan quotes a Confederate general as saying, "We were lavish of blood in those days, and it was thought to be a great thing to charge a battery of artillery or an earthwork lined with infantry." Since the Mexican war, rifles had been developed that were much more accurate over a longer range, and quicker to reload. The fat conical bullets they fired ripped much nastier holes in flesh and bone than either the musket ball of previous wars or the higher-velocity but lower-caliber bullets that would be used in World War I. So the attackers were mowed down in enormous numbers. Sometimes those who happened randomly not to be killed kept charging until they were able to chase the dug-in ones out of their holes and start killing them, but more often the tempest of iron and lead prevailed. As Confederate general D. H. Hill said of a particularly egregious but by no means unrepresentative instance of this, "It was not war. It was murder."

Lee did have a proactive agenda. And he had Stonewall Jackson. On a horse—Little Sorrel, his shambling, sorry-looking "dun cob"—Jackson cut a ludicrous figure. He had *huge* outturned feet. He wore a ratty old cap. His voice, remembered a fellow West Point cadet, "was thin and feminine—almost squeaky—while his utterances were quick, jerky and sententious."

James I. Robertson Jr., Jackson's now-standard biographer, insists that the stories of Stonewall's constantly sucking on lemons are just myth—that he enjoyed all fruit, especially peaches. But he did have dietary quirks: For instance, he fended off his "arch-enemy," dyspepsia, by buying fresh bread and then laying it out on a shelf to get just stale enough, as timed by his pocket watch, before he ate it. Every now and then—for instance, during his first interview with Lee, back before the war—he would unself-consciously hold one arm straight up in the air for a while to lighten it—he felt it was heavier than the other. Usually his expression was wooden, but in battle his eyes lit up. It may well be true that, as F. Scott Fitzgerald famously observed, "The test of a first-rate intelligence is the ability to hold two opposed ideas in the mind at the same time, and still retain the ability to function," but there is also something to be said—even without reference to how raggedly Fitzgerald functioned—for single-mindedness. In warfare, particularly. Jackson, Mary Chesnut told her diary after hearing him described by another general, "was a one-idea man." Orphaned at an early age, Jackson took God as his father, heaven as his destination, and killing enemy soldiers as his duty. Once, when a colonel under him expressed regret that his men had killed three Union soldiers whose gallantry had been conspicuous, Jackson said, "No, Colonel. Shoot them all. I don't want them to be brave."

When Sam Watkins first came under Jackson's command, he and his comrades reached the verge of mutiny. Icicles were hanging from the men's clothing as they marched: "My feet peeled off like a peeled onion on that march, and I have not recovered from its effects to this day." When Jackson would ride past a regiment, "they would take occasion, *sotto voce*, to abuse him, and call him 'Fool Tom Jackson,' and loud enough for him to hear." But Watkins, who was no fool himself except to the extent that war distorted everything, came to admire Jackson under the circumstances. "He did his duty himself and was ever at his post, and he expected and demanded of everybody to do the same thing. He would have a man shot at the drop of a hat, and drop it himself. The first army order that was ever read to us after being attached to his corps, was the shooting to death by musketry of two men who had stopped on the battlefield to carry off a wounded comrade." Jackson simplified things. "Stonewall," the nickname he won at First Manassas, was less appropriate than "Thunderbolt" would have been, and it was perfectly clear to Jackson that his lightning aggressiveness was in the service of God. Men under him—including Pvt. Robert E. Lee Jr.—fought purposefully and hard.

Ever since First Manassas, Jackson had been insisting that the South must seize the initiative, go on the offensive, invade the North. Lee was of the same mind. He reinforced Jackson in the Shenandoah Valley. There Jackson confounded greatly superior forces with swift tactical moves to win battle after battle. Then Lee brought him to bear east of Richmond. The subsequent series of battles, known as the Seven Days, was badly coordinated all around. Jackson, uncharacteristically (he was probably exhausted), kept failing to get his army into position on time. Lee, uncharacteristically (it seemed at the time), had fire in his eye. On the second day things were going badly for the Confederates. Lee, observing the action as artillery shells exploded around him, noticed that President Davis had arrived with a civilian entourage. "Who is all this army and what is it doing here?" Lee demanded. "This is no place for it." Davis and his fellow officials got out of the way. On the third day, insanely gallant gray waves breached the Union's position, but at a price of 7,993 Confederate casualties to the Union's 6,827. On the sixth day McClellan's army might have been effectively destroyed, but it managed to withdraw because, as Lee angrily exclaimed, "I cannot have my orders carried out!" On the seventh day, at Malvern Hill, Lee ordered one of those frontal assaults on an unassailable position that resulted in useless slaughter, in this case of Confederates. And yet when the dust settled McClellan had been pushed back. He had left behind lots of direly needed arms, wagons, and supplies. Richmond was no longer imminently threatened. Lee was a hero of the South.

Now a new Union force under Gen. John Pope assailed northern Virginia, and McClellan moved to join him. Though outnumbered, Lee persisted in audacity, dividing his army to send Jackson against Pope's rear and Longstreet around to the south. A smarter adversary could have broken both wings, but Pope concentrated on Jackson while Longstreet, screened by mountains, advanced toward his exposed left flank. Longstreet proceeded with characteristic caution bordering on reluctance, and Lee, with characteristic indulgence of his subordinates' discretion, did not push him. "I strive to make my plans as good as my human skill allows," Lee told a foreign observer, "but on the day of battle, I lay the fate of my army in the hands of God; it is my generals' turn to perform their duty." Jackson's men were a stone wall, and then, when Longstreet was at last ready to sweep in, he did so with characteristic effectiveness. He and Jackson attacked Pope from two sides, driving the Federals away from the Manassas (or Bull Run) field for the second time. Lee's men had not eaten in three days. Casualties: 9,500 Confederate, 14,500 Union. It was after this battle that Lee fell and put both of his hands out of commission. McClellan withdrew across the Potomac to defend Washington, and Pope was sent to Minnesota to fight the Sioux. Lee fed his troops, mostly on green corn, and invaded Maryland.

Lee's generals squabbled among themselves. A Union soldier found a copy of Lee's overall invasion plan wrapped around three cigars. Lee's troops were described by a Maryland resident who saw them on the march: "When I say they were hungry, I convey no impression of the gaunt starvation that looked from their cavernous eyes. . . . Never were want and exhaustion more visibly put before my eyes, and that they could march or fight at all seemed incredible." Morale and discipline were low, but those who stayed in ranks had the humor to sing "Maryland, My Maryland." They struck a Maryland boy named Leighton Parks as "the dirtiest men I ever saw, a most ragged, lean and hungry set of wolves. Yet there was a dash about them that the Northern men lacked." Those were the hard core. As many as half of the army had deserted—though some of these would return after going home to check things at the farm.

Lee had in mind a clean invasion, with no disturbance of civilians. He issued a proclamation inviting Maryland's populace to spontaneously free themselves from the "foreign yoke" of Union and join the cause. "The army will respect your choice, whatever it may be; and, while the Southern people will rejoice to welcome you to your natural position among them, they will only welcome you when you come by your own free will." His men and horses and mules could forage off the countryside—northern Virginia's having been exhausted—but he issued stern orders against pillaging. Many of the troops were too hungry and too independently resourceful, however, to obey. At Antietam, Lee himself came upon a straggler carrying a stolen pig and ordered him shot. The man's more immediate commander, Jackson, was so short of bodies at the time that he sent the man to the front lines instead (he survived). Young Rob Lee came to his father's tent holding the shreds of leather that had been his shoes. Could he get a new pair? he wondered.

"Have the men in your company received permission to draw shoes yet?"

"No, sir; I believe not yet."

"Then go back to your battery, my boy, and wait till they have."

Indeed, a great many Maryland ladies came to the headquarters eager to meet the dashing Confederate commanders of whom they had heard so much. Maryland did not want, however, to be liberated. And Lee's army was highly vulnerable. Lee knew this (for one thing, he'd been informed by a spy that the order found wrapped around the cigars had been conveyed to McClellan), and so did Abraham Lincoln, who urged McClellan to smash Lee's overextended army while he had the chance. But McClellan—highly popular among his troops because he was so loath to risk their lives—could never quite get over the suspicion that Lee had something up his sleeve. How *could* he be so audacious otherwise? What Lee had up his sleeve was McClellan's awe of him, and the unreasoning faith that Lee's army, what was left of it, had in him. Even so, no one has ever come up with a convincing explanation of why in mid-September 1862 Lee took up a position on hills along Antietam Creek, with only one narrow route of escape back over the Potomac into Virginia, and dared McClellan to attack. The great Battle of Antietam (or Sharpsburg) was the war's bloodiest. "Great God!" wrote a Confederate to his wife, "it looks like they are going to kill all the men in battle before they stop." More than ten thousand, between a fourth and a third, of the Confederates were killed, wounded, or missing. But McClellan committed his forces tentatively (losing more than twelve thousand casualties even so) and did not press his advantage. Lee, marshaling his ravaged corps and divisions brilliantly to meet each Union thrust, was determined to fight on, but McClellan had had enough. Its honor intact, the Army of Northern Virginia withdrew to its home turf with a Pyrrhic draw.

Near Winchester, Virginia, Lee's aide Col. A. L. Long began to set up headquarters on an amenable farmer's large shady lawn. The farmer offered Lee the use of rooms in the house. Lee not only declined the chance to rest indoors, preferring his small tent, but insisted that Long move everything off the lawn. Long found a field so rocky that it was hard to ride on, much less sleep. "This is better than the yard," Lee said. "We will not disturb those good people." Whereas Federals had "foully polluted" both Arlington and Rooney's White House by moving into them, Lee wouldn't even accept freely offered hospitality. A British observer found Lee's pointed rejection of a roof and a soft bed endearing, adding that Lee "is a person that, wherever seen, whether in a castle or a hovel, alone or in a crowd, must at once attract attention as being a splendid specimen of an English gentleman, with one of the most rarely handsome faces I ever saw."

"I believe my chief was most anxious to recross into

Maryland but was persuaded by his principal advisors that the condition of the army did not warrant such a move," wrote Walter Taylor, his aide. During the autumn of 1862 Lee rested his army and got them better fed and clothed. Morale improved and deserters returned. One day in October he read his mail, then called Taylor into his tent to assign him administrative chores. Taylor went away, but returned unexpectedly. He found Lee "overcome with grief, an open letter in his hands." Before instructing Taylor, Lee had learned that his daughter Annie—Ann Carter Lee, the one named for his mother, the only one of his children whose nickname hadn't stuck—had died of typhoid fever at twenty-three. Shyer and gentler than her sisters, she had a birthmark on her right cheek ("Little Raspberry," Lee had called her in a letter home reacting to news of her birth), and a childhood accident with scissors had left her blind and deformed on that side. In an old photograph of sisters and cousins, one is probably Annie because whereas the others face us, looking rather relaxed for camera subjects of the time, she stands, looking pretty but rigid, in left profile. "His army demanded his first thought and care," wrote Taylor. "Who can tell with what anguish of soul he endeavored to control himself, and to maintain a calm exterior, and who can estimate the intense effort necessary to still the heart filled to overflowing with tenderest emotions?"

"To know that I shall never see her again on earth," Lee wrote to his wife, "that her place in our circle, which I always had hoped one day to enjoy, is forever vacant, is agonizing in the extreme." However, "It is a great comfort to me to know that she is relieved from the pain, anxiety and suffering of this world."

Soon thereafter he also sent Mary a message for a young woman of their acquaintance who had requested that he send her a proxy kiss, via two of his officers that she knew. He would love to send the kiss, Lee wrote, but "when I look at [the officers] and think of her, nature revolts!" He managed a brief visit to Mary in Richmond. While there he rode past the house of friends and saw the family's comely daughter sitting on the front steps coolly receiving the attentions of a young swain. Lee dismounted, walked to the steps, bent to kiss the belle, and said to her suitor, "Wouldn't you like to do that, sir?" Then he got back on his horse and rode away.

On the war front Lee's first priority was to keep the Yankees out of Richmond. Lincoln relieved McClellan from command of the Army of the Potomac, replacing him with Ambrose E. Burnside. "I fear they may continue to make these changes till they find some one I don't understand," Lee remarked. Not yet. He figured, and Jeb Stuart's scouting confirmed, that Burnside would attempt to prove his forthrightness to Lincoln by making an unimaginative beeline toward Richmond. He would have to cross the Rappahannock River at Fredericksburg, Virginia, in whose general vicinity, according to legend, Washington had thrown a silver dollar across the river. Lee moved to stop him.

Burnside's artillery already controlled the town of Fredericksburg. Burnside himself was ensconced at Chatham, Lee's late mother-in-law's family estate, where George Washington had courted Martha and Lee had courted Mary. As the Federals constructed pontoon bridges for the river crossing, Confederate sharpshooters in the town picked them off. Union artillery responded by reducing much of the small town to rubble. "Those people delight to destroy the weak and those who can make no defense," Lee exclaimed. "It just suits them!" When those people finally got across the icy river, they lived up to Lee's opinion of them, merrily looting and vandalizing what was left of the homes of Fredericksburg.

Lee meanwhile had set up a seven-mile defensive line along a series of hills just beyond the town. He wanted Burnside to attack him here, and Burnside obliged—in fact he concentrated on the strong position's strongest point, a steep hill called Marye's Heights. Lee's artillery commander, Edward Porter Alexander, placed his guns to such advantage that he reckoned "a chicken could not live" on the open approach to the heights. A heavy fog rolled in. But then it lifted, revealing a mass of blue, half again as many men as Lee's. Alexander's cannons opened, and so did the riflemen of Jackson and Longstreet. Many of these were barefoot and without coats or bedding in the mid-December cold, but they were hard as nails. "Come on, blue belly! Bring them boots and blankets!" they cried.

Some eleven thousand Union men were cut down. Confederate casualties were less than half that. It was while this one-sided butchery went on that Lee—after not turning a hair when a bit of falling ordnance scattered him with dirt—made what would become his most quoted remark: "It is well that war is so terrible, or we should grow too fond of it."

"What luck some people have," Gen. Joe Johnston grumbled after learning of Lee's victory. "Nobody will ever come to attack me in such a place."

Burnside wanted to send his men against the hill again the next day, and Lee hoped he would, but Burnside's commanders talked him out of it. In the night underdressed Confederates stripped Yankee bodies, which lay, according to an observer, "one without a head, there one without legs, yonder a head and legs without a trunk; everywhere horrible expressions, fear, rage, agony, madness, torture; lying in pools of blood, lying with heads half buried in mud, with fragments of shell sticking in oozing brain, with bullet holes all over the puffed limbs." According to Shelby Foote, one Confederate scavenger was pulling a boot off what he took to be a dead man when the man lifted his head. "Beg pardon, sir," said the Confederate. "I thought you had gone above."

Lee set up winter headquarters at Fredericksburg. The weather was nasty. Burnside attempted to turn Lee's flank by moving upriver but bogged down in the mud. Lincoln replaced him with "Fighting Joe" Hooker. Lee occupied himself with details involved in the emancipation of his father-in-law's slaves. "As regards the servants," he wrote to Mary:

Those that are hired out can soon be settled. They can be furnished with their free papers & hire themselves out. Those on the farms I will issue free papers to as soon as I can see that they can get a support. As long as they remain on the farms they must continue as they are. Any who wish to leave can do so. The men could no doubt find homes, but what are the women & children to do? . . . I shall not issue any free passes to the people while they are on the farms. As long as they remain there they must work as usual. I will be willing to devote the net proceeds of their labour for the year to their future establishment. Those at Arlington & Alexandria I cannot now reach. They are already free & when I can get to them I will give them their papers.

A few days later, on January 1, 1863, Abraham Lincoln's proclamation, which he had first announced in the wake of the good news that Lee had been stopped at Antietam, became official: "That . . . all persons held as slaves within any State or designated part of a State, the people whereof shall then be in rebellion against the United States, shall be then, thenceforward, and forever free." Lee started paying his servant, Perry, and his cook, George, $8.20 a month each. (In Confederate money, whose value was rapidly depreciating. A private soldier made $11.00, but he couldn't count on getting it every month. Just before the war Lee had written to Rooney, "I fear I shall have to purchase a servant. I find it almost impossible to hire one. . . . At present I have a boy belonging to Major Marlin for whom I pay $20 per month.") It bothered him that Reuben and Parks, two of the slaves he had farmed out before the war for rebelling against his authority, and another man, Harrison, couldn't be located, and consequently couldn't be given the liberation papers he had spent so much time on. Presumably these men had managed to liberate themselves without papers, but Lee urged Custis to do all he could to find them, and when he heard, halfway through the war, that Reuben had died, he succinctly expressed sorrow.

To his wife Lee wrote, "[W]hat a cruel thing is war." To Mildred he wrote, "You must write to me sometimes you precious child, without waiting for me to reply. I have little time for writing to my children. But you must be sure that I am always thinking of you, always wishing to see you. I have only received two letters from you & replied to both." To son Custis, "If my pants are done, will you give them to Mr. Thomas, the bearer, who will bring them up tomorrow. . . . I am in my last pair, and very sensitive, fearful of an accident." To his wife, "As for my health I suppose I shall never be better. Old age and sorrow is wearing me away, & constant anxiety and labour, day & night. . . . You forget how much writing, talking & thinking I have to do, when you complain of the interval between my letters. . . . There are but two pairs left of my thinnest drawers, & I doubt whether anything can be done for them." His health got so bad in March that doctors, "tapping me all over like an old steam boiler before condemning it," persuaded him to move into a nearby family's house. Feeble, feverish, and in pain, he was bedridden for weeks—probably suffering from angina pectoris, from which he never entirely recovered.

But as the weather improved he was up and around, and his most daring generalship was ahead of him. No thanks to the Confederate government, which seemed incapable of providing the food, clothing, and additional troops he desperately needed. "Nothing now," he wrote to son Custis,

can arrest during the [Lincoln] administration the most desolating war that was ever practiced, except a revolution
among their people. Nothing can produce a revolution except systematic success on our part. What has our Congress
done to meet the exigency? . . . As far as I know, concocted
bills to excuse a certain class of men from taking service. . . .
I hope Congress will define what makes a man a citizen of a
State. For some apply for regiments of States in which they
were born, when it suits their purpose, while others apply
for regiments of States in which they live, or have married,
or visited, or where they have relatives . . . , but never when
the regiments of these States are in active service.

During the winter Hooker had been, as Lee wrote to
Agnes, "trying what frightening will do. He runs out his guns
starts his wagons and troops up & down the river & creates an
excitement generally. Our men look on in wonder, give a
cheer, & all again subsides 'in statu quo ante bellum.'"

Stonewall Jackson's wife, Anna, and their baby came to
camp for a visit, something the hobbled Mary Lee never did.
Jackson rarely let little Julia out of his arms, except when she
cried. Then, according to Mrs. Jackson, he would put her in
her cradle and wait, "with as much coolness and determination as if he were directing a battle," until she stopped crying.
Then he would hold her again. But on April 29 Jackson had
to tell his family good-bye, because Hooker had moved to
live up to his nickname. He had taken a large force around to
Lee's left, crossing the river west of Fredericksburg, and sent a
second force of cavalry at him head-on. Lee sent a division
commanded by Richard H. Anderson to meet the leftward
attack at the village of Chancellorsville. When Anderson got

there, he was forced to pull back and dig in. Lee left 10,000 men under Jubal Early to hold off 23,000 Federals at Fredericksburg, and took his 43,000 other men around to meet a general attack by Hooker's 73,000 east of Chancellorsville. It was madly dangerous, splitting his army this way, but it was his only chance. In fact, he had just begun to split.

Hooker was a hell of a fellow, handsome and arrogant. (There is a persistent belief that "hooker" became a synonym for prostitute because of Fighting Joe's taste for scarlet women. This is untrue, but only because the term was already in use before he came along.) Hooker knew how to fight, and he knew how to party. But Lee spooked him. He was determined not to make Burnside's mistake, of wasting his main strength head-on against a strong Confederate position, but Lee's position here was tenuous. For no conceivable reason other than Leephobia, Hooker instead of pressing his great advantage pulled back to let Lee attack him.

Lee personally scouted around to his right. It didn't look good.

Jackson went into his tent. All around officers were chattering. "Hush!" cried an aide. "The General is praying!" Silence fell. Jackson emerged looking serene. He rode to confer with Lee. The two of them sat on a log. "How can we get at those people?" Lee asked. Jeb Stuart rode up. He had scouted around to the left, and found Hooker's flank there (his right) "up in the air"—unprotected. Lee decided to split again, by sending Jackson off to attack that flank. They slept on it. The next morning they looked at a map and had the following famous conversation:

"What do you propose to do?" asked Lee.

"Go around here," said Jackson, pointing to Hooker's exposed flank.

"What do you propose to make this movement with?"

"With my whole corps."

"What will you leave me?"

"The divisions of Anderson and McLaws."

"Well, go on."

Jackson took off into the thick tangle of stunted pines and undergrowth called the Wilderness with 26,000 men, leaving Lee with 17,000 looking at Hooker's 73,000. Jackson's men thrashed through brush and jumped over logs for twelve hours in strict silence, as Lee feinted back and forth for twelve hours. The Federal right was napping and cooking supper. Suddenly deer, wild turkeys, and rabbits came rushing through their camp. Some of the unsuspecting Bluecoats, delighted to have game for supper, ran to catch the animals. Then they heard the Rebel yell. Then they saw, as one of the Confederates described it, "a solid wall of gray, forcing their way through the timber and bearing down upon them like an irresistible avalanche." Hearing the noise of Jackson tearing into Hooker's weak side, Lee attacked from the front. His army had gone from being caught between the jaws of a greatly superior force to catching the bigger jaw between smaller, quicker, more audacious jaws, like a little feist dog getting his uppers and lowers into a mastiff's snout and shaking him.

But that night, after pressing farther ahead through the thickets, Jackson's gray wave was disorganized, losing momentum. Jackson and his staff rode to the front to reconnoiter. In the confusion, a Confederate regiment fired on them.

Jackson took three bullets to the left shoulder and forearm and the right hand. Little Sorrel ran away. "All my wounds are by my own men," murmured Jackson, bewildered for once. As he was being carried off the field, an artillery barrage caused him to be dropped twice on the bad shoulder, rupturing an artery. Although he had given up liquor years before because, he said, he liked it, now he asked for spirits. He was given whiskey and water. He upbraided an officer who wanted to pull back from the front, and then he applied himself to suffering stoically.

Lee was informed. He fell silent, then exclaimed: "Ah, Captain, any victory is dearly bought that deprives us of the services of General Jackson even for a short time." Apparently that is the way he talked. When the messenger began to describe the wounds in detail, Lee's response was less measured: "Oh, don't talk about it!"

He sent Jackson a message saying in part, "I should have chosen for the good of the country to have been disabled in your stead," and giving him credit for the victory. "General Lee is very kind," said Jackson, whose left arm had been amputated, "but he should give the praise to God."

Stuart put on a new uniform with gold lace, gilt buttons, a dancing black-and-red plume on his hat, and a bright red artillery sash to replace his yellow cavalry one, and took over Jackson's command. "Remember Jackson!" cried the men. At one point Stuart leaped his horse over a breastwork and led a charge that captured a position from which artillery fired a shell that hit a pillar of a house where Hooker was standing and dislodged a chunk that knocked Hooker silly. At one point Stuart—in his new blue uniform—rode right at a line of

Federal troops that had opened fire on his men and commanded them to stop shooting. This confused them just long enough for Stuart's men to regroup, and Stuart himself rode back to his men through—you guessed it—a hail of bullets. Hooker was whipped.

Lee rode to the front of his victorious army. A staff officer recalled:

> One long, unbroken cheer, in which the feeble cry of those who lay helpless on the earth blended with the strong voices of those who still fought, rose high above the roar of battle, and hailed the presence of the victorious chief. He sat in the full realization of all that soldiers dream of—triumph; and as I looked upon him in the complete fruition of the success. . . . I thought that it must have been from such a scene that men in ancient days rose to the dignity of gods.

"What a head, what a head!" one of the men cried. "See that glorious head! God bless it, God bless it!"

Why do I feel obliged to deprive Lee of this heady moment? Not that a man of his chronic ambivalence would have admitted, even to himself, that it was heady. It wasn't as good as his father's war. Bigger *spectacle,* yes, but that's just it. Harry had also been adept at this sort of tactics, splitting his smaller force to hit the flanks of a dazzled larger one. Robert might be seen as nifty David versus stuffy Goliath, or maybe we should call it canny Brer Rabbit versus lumbering Brer Bear. Except—how can we identify Brer Rabbit, the trickster figure who outsmarts the power in African-American lore, with a general whose cause entailed slavery? (Uncle Remus, the slave who told the Brer Rabbit stories in Joel Chandler Harris's versions, never told how Brer Rabbit got unstuck from the Tar Baby that entrapped him; Uncle Remus never got free.) And Harry's violence was small-scale, hands-on, personal-skill-intensive, low-casualty, all-for-one-and-one-for-all. Even in wily victory Robert was an old guy sending masses of independent-natured young yeomen to their largely luck-of-the-draw deaths in a kind of blast furnace whose direct heat he had never experienced and never would. He knew his father's shame, but not his glory.

And while Lee was being hoorayed, Hooker was ordering a retreat across the Rappahannock, which had become the de facto border between North and South. Lee stormed at the officer who brought news of Hooker's escape: "This is the way you young men always do. You allow those people to get away. I tell you what to do, and you don't do it!" A great tactical victory, but not telling strategically, and as usual, Pyrrhic. Casualties amounted to more than 20 percent of Lee's army. Jackson's wounds became infected, and he contracted pneumonia.

Anna Jackson reached her husband's bedside in time for him to tell her, "You are one of the most precious little wives in the world." (He'd had another one, equally sweet, who died in childbirth, and whose inseparable sister, whose company he cherished, he would have married thereafter, had Presbyterian dogma not forbidden it.)

"Before this day closes," Anna told him, "you will be with the blessed Saviour in His glory." Years before, she had confided in a letter that their neighbors would never dream how demonstratively affectionate her husband was. The two of them, behind closed doors so the neighbors wouldn't know, would dance the polka.

"I will be an infinite gainer to be translated," Jackson told his wife. Despite great pain he declined brandy, so that he might be alert to the end. And evidently his last words actually were, "Let us cross over the river, and rest in the shade of the trees."

Lee had not visited his greatest lieutenant during the eight days he lay dying—the burdens of command, presumably. High-born Lee and hillbilly Jackson had hit it off instinctively but almost tacitly. They were not comrades. After learning of Jackson's death, however, Lee summoned a chaplain, in whose company he wept.

CHAPTER EIGHT

Now, AS THE SUMMER of 1863 approached, Confederate forces were being steadily beaten back everywhere outside Virginia. Most crucially, Grant with sixty thousand troops had Vicksburg, Mississippi, defended by half that many, under siege. The people were reduced to eating rats. Although the loss of Vicksburg would give the Union control of all the Mississippi River and effectively end the South's chances of winning the war outright, Lee didn't want to send Virginian reinforcements there. He proposed, and Davis approved, an advance into Pennsylvania. There was nothing left for men or horses or mules to eat in the fields of northern Virginia, and Lee saw a decisive victory in the North as the Confederacy's only chance of getting out of the war intact. He also urged Jefferson Davis to "give all the encouragement we can, consistently with truth, to the rising peace party of the North"— the Democrats, whose appeal to war-weary voters offered them a good chance of taking the presidency from Lincoln.

Without Jackson, Lee would have to rely more heavily on his other corps commander, Gen. James "Pete" Longstreet, who was staunchly effective under fire but slow to get under way, and who preferred—sensibly, in this war—to take the defensive. Longstreet and his half of the army had missed Chancellorsville because Lee had allowed him the discretion to head south looking for supplies. Lee had hinted to Longstreet that he wished he would come back, but he was strangely reluctant to *order* him back, and Longstreet had gotten involved in indecisive action around Suffolk, Virginia. Now Lee reorganized his two corps, which had been commanded by Jackson and Longstreet, into three smaller corps under Longstreet; Richard S. Ewell, who had only one leg; and A. P. Hill, a fine commander who was suffering from complications of gonorrhea. Lee also enlarged Jeb Stuart's separate cavalry command. Longstreet, perhaps feeling diminished by the reorganization, explored the possibility of being assigned to someone else's command. Lee called Longstreet his "Old War Horse," but he never took to him the way he did to Jackson, and Longstreet felt that.

Walter Taylor, the aide, wrote of Lee to his future wife, "I might serve under him for ten years to come and couldn't *love* him at the end of that period. . . . Ah! But he is a queer old genius. I suppose it is so with all great men."

How much could Lee love or be loved by any individual outside his family, in a way to satisfy anyone less self-sufficient than Jackson? He certainly expressed fondness for his former West Point student Stuart. Before the Battles of the Seven Days, without informing anyone what he was up to except by way of a hint to Lee, Stuart had taken twelve hundred men and ridden entirely around McClellan's army, covering a hundred miles in just over three days while suffering only one casualty (whose body was brought back for a roses-on-the-bier funeral that inspired a poem and a painting whose popularity swept the South). In the process Stuart's merry men not only discovered, as at Chancellorsville, a Federal flank "in the air," but also evaded or scattered several Federal outfits that tried to stop them, destroyed millions of dollars' worth of Federal stores and property, gorged on Federal figs and champagne, built a bridge to cross the swollen Chicka-hominy and then burned it just before the arrival of pursuers (who, as Stuart put it in his report, were at his heels "armed with the fury of a tigress robbed of her whelps"), captured 165 prisoners and 260 horses and mules, and sent a Federal supply train speeding toward a Federal base with a dead engi-neer at the throttle. As much as Jackson, Stuart was the heart and soul of Lee's mythic invincibility.

"He is my eyes," said Lee. Stuart sought, and usually man-aged, to "own" the space between Lee's army and its oppo-nents, scouting the enemy and keeping the enemy from adequately scouting Lee. In this war of infantry charges and long-range barrages, cavalry couldn't provide the sort of slashing aggressive force that had often been decisive during the Revolution, but Stuart must have made Lee think of the young Light-Horse Harry. And maybe he made Lee think what kind of young hero he himself might have been, if the war in Mexico (where Lee was Scott's eyes) had amounted to more.

Lee and Stuart had much in common. Stuart's was an old Virginia family of the cavalier class, but his father had wasted his inheritance and left the family hard up, and his mother was stern. Mindful of what the father's bonhomie had cost her, she made young J. E. B. vow never to take a drink. Stuart, like Lee, was a Rebel not because he favored secession but because he loved Virginia. He also loved to dance and flirt, and he was an outspoken servant of the will of God.

But Stuart got much more of a bang out of life than Lee did. At West Point he earned *lots* of demerits. Like Lee he married a well-born woman who was no beauty; but unlike Mary Lee, Flora Stuart was vivacious, a fine horsewoman who could also shoot and play the guitar. Whereas Lee had chased Indians fruitlessly and let them depress him, Stuart had fought them hand-to-hand. Whereas the self-denying Lee's promotions during his prime had been slow, the self-advancing Stuart rose in the first year of the war from first lieutenant to brigadier general. Whereas Lee was stuck with settling his father-in-law's encumbered estate, Stuart heartily hated his father-in-law for siding with the Union and had the satisfaction of embarrassing him in battle. The father-in-law commanded cavalry that should have caught Stuart on his way around McClellan.

Like Grant, Stuart was called "Beauty" by his West Point classmates, but in Stuart's case it was because his big nose, prim-looking lips, and receding chin made him so strikingly unprepossessing. So he grew a voluminous ginger beard, which covered his lower face, balanced his nose, and set off his intensely blue eyes. And he dressed himself up—not in pointedly plain elegance like Lee, but as at Chancellorsville, flamboyantly. Whereas Lee seemed to pride himself on making do with short rations, in Stuart's camp there always seemed to be plenty of food and eggnog. During the war he was accompanied not by a pet hen but by a pet raccoon, three black minstrels, and a Robin Hood's band of eccentric companions—like the six-foot-two, 250-pound Prussian soldier of fortune Heros von Borcke, who would go out of his way to find bullets to dodge, and a Corporal Hagan, whom a fellow soldier described as "a very giant in frame" with "grotesque fierceness," a "voice as hoarse as distant thunder," and "an abnormal tendency to develop hair." Stuart got to be such friends with the very dissimilar Jackson that once, on arriving in Jackson's camp in the middle of the night, he climbed into the sleeping Stonewall's bunk and contended with him for the covers. The next morning Jackson said, "I'm always glad to have you, but you must not get into my bed with your boots and spurs on and ride me around like a cavalry horse all night." On other occasions Stuart kidded Jackson until the latter blushed like a schoolgirl. When Stuart learned during the war of *his* daughter's death, he fell into von Borcke's arms and sobbed.

Many an older commander might have regarded Stuart sourly, clamped down on him out of envy. But it was Lee's way to give his officers leeway. Maybe he should have been stricter with Stuart: Jeb had started signing letters "Knight of the Golden Spurs," or "K.G.S." He was a major general now, and although a Minié ball had carried off half his mustache, people were writing songs about him. After Antietam he had ridden all the way around McClellan's army *again,* improving his record to eighteen hundred men traveling 126 miles in thirty-six hours with no casualties and penetrating into Pennsylvania; but this, known as the Chambersburg raid, was more swashbuckling than significant. He needed to top himself.

He mounted a review of some of his troops, and it went

so splendidly that a couple of weeks later he staged a gala review of all 9,536 of them, with cannons shooting off, horses prancing in time to band music, ranks charging at the gallop in precision, cheering horsemen stretched out over a mile and a half, ladies strewing flowers. Lee was unable to attend that review, so Stuart laid on another one for him three days later. By this time the troops were pageant-weary.

As Stuart's people were getting mobilized to begin screening Lee's advance to the north, Hooker's cavalry pulled off a surprise predawn attack at Brandy Station, scene of all those reviews. Stuart sprang out of bed and threw together a response that prevented the Federal cavalry from destroying his—in fact the Confederates, as usual in Virginia, killed and wounded more Yankees than vice versa—but the trickster had been tricked. He'd opened himself to criticism among the ranks and in the Southern press. "If he is to be the 'eyes and ears of the army,' we would advise him to see more and be seen less," said the *Richmond Enquirer.* Lee sent him a message of less than effusive reassurance.

That it should come to this! Stuart *needing* reassurance. But what may have hurt Stuart the most was that Brandy Station was the largest cavalry battle ever in North America, and objectively it was small potatoes: fewer than a thousand casualties on each side (one of the wounded was Rooney Lee), and both sides pulling back at the sight of infantry reserves. Jeb Stuart, young enough to be Lee's son and a bold-enough dragoon to have been Lee's father, was marginal in the bloody scheme of things. He wasn't used to incurring casualties. Capt. Will Farley, the sport who had ridden alongside the speeding Union supply train and shot the engineer dead during the first circumnavigation of McClellan, got his leg torn off at Brandy Station by a random piece of shell. As he lay dying he asked for his leg, hugged it, and joked, "It is an old friend, gentlemen." Cavalier drollery. As the inelegant Grant and Sherman would prove in the long run, this war was not personal exploits and dashing camaraderie, but hell.

We come now to Gettysburg, Pennsylvania. The high-water mark of the Confederacy, it used to be called, before scholarly analysis left that ringing phrase in the dustbin of history. More likely, the Confederacy's prospects had been receding since Antietam. But for William Faulkner in *Intruder in the Dust* it was Southern manhood's turning point:

> For every Southern boy fourteen years old, not once but whenever he wants it, there is the instant when it's still not yet two o'clock on the July afternoon in 1863 . . . the furled flags are already loosened to break out and Pickett himself with his long oiled ringlets and his hat in one hand probably and his sword in the other looking up the hill waiting for Longstreet to give the word and it's all in the balance, it hasn't happened yet . . . there is still time for it not to begin against that position and those circumstances . . . yet it's going to begin, we all know that, we have come too far and with too much at stake and that moment doesn't even need a fourteen-year-old boy to think *this time. Maybe this time* with all this much to lose and all this much to gain: Pennsylvania, Maryland, the world, the golden dome of Washington itself to crown with desperate and unbelievable victory the gamble . . . or the moment in 1492 when somebody thought *This is it;* the absolute edge of no return, to turn

back now and make home or sail irrevocably on and either find land or plunge over the world's roaring rim.

Fourteen-year-old Southern boys have by and large moved on to other concerns since 1948, when *Intruder in the Dust* was published, and even then Faulkner's demographic brush was broad, especially considering how many fourteen-year-old Southern boys were descendants of slaves. But the days of July 1–3, 1863, do still stand among the most horrific and formative in American history. And the battle was a watershed for Lee.

Lincoln had given up on Joe Hooker, put Gen. George G. Meade in command of the Army of the Potomac, and sent him to stop Lee's invasion of Pennsylvania. Since Stuart's scouting operation had been uncharacteristically out of touch, Lee wasn't sure where Meade's army was. Lee had actually advanced farther north than Gettysburg, when he learned that Meade was south of him, threatening his supply lines. So Lee swung back in that direction. On June 30 a Confederate brigade, pursuing the report that there were shoes to be had in Gettysburg, ran into Federal cavalry west of town, and withdrew. On July 1 a larger Confederate force returned, engaged Meade's advance force, and pushed it back through the town—to the fishhook-shaped heights comprising Cemetery Hill, Cemetery Ridge, Little Round Top, and Round Top. It was almost a rout, until Gen. O. O. Howard, to whom Lee as West Point superintendent had been kind when Howard was an unpopular cadet, and Gen. Winfield Scott Hancock, named for Lee's old patron, rallied the Federals and held the high ground.

Excellent ground to defend from. That evening Longstreet urged Lee not to attack, but to swing around to the south, get between Meade and Washington, and find a strategically even better defensive position, against which the Federals might feel obliged to mount one of those frontal assaults that virtually always lost in this war. Still not having heard from Stuart, Lee felt he might have numerical superiority for once. "No," he said, "the enemy is there, and I am going to attack him there."

The next morning, Lee set in motion a two-part offensive: Ewell's corps was to pin down the enemy's right flank, on Culp's Hill and Cemetery Hill, while Longstreet's, with a couple of extra divisions, would hit the left flank—believed to be exposed—on Cemetery Ridge. To get there Longstreet would have to make a long march under cover. Longstreet mounted a sulky objection, but Lee was adamant. And wrong.

Lee didn't know that in the night Meade had managed by forced marches to concentrate nearly his entire army at Lee's front, and had deployed it skillfully—his left flank was now extended to Little Round Top, nearly three-quarters of a mile south of where Lee thought it was. The disgruntled Longstreet, never one to rush into anything, and confused to find the left flank further left than expected, didn't begin his assault until three-thirty that afternoon. It nearly prevailed anyway, but at last was beaten gorily back. Although the two-pronged offensive was ill-coordinated, and the Federal artillery had knocked out the Confederate guns to the north before Ewell attacked, Ewell's infantry came tantalizingly close to taking Cemetery Hill, but a counterattack forced them to retreat.

On the third morning, July 3, Lee's plan was roughly the same, but Meade seized the initiative by pushing forward on his right and seizing Culp's Hill, which the Confederates held. So Lee was forced to improvise. He decided to strike straight ahead, at Meade's heavily fortified midsection. Confederate artillery would soften it up, and Longstreet would direct a frontal assault across a mile of open ground against the center of Missionary Ridge. Again Longstreet objected; again Lee wouldn't listen. The Confederate artillery exhausted all its shells ineffectively, so was unable to support the assault—which has gone down in history as Pickett's charge because General Pickett's division absorbed the worst of the horrible bloodbath it turned into.

Lee's idolators strained after the war to shift the blame, but the consensus today is that Lee managed the battle badly. Each supposed major blunder of his subordinates—General Ewell's failure to take the high ground of Cemetery Hill on July 1, Stuart's getting out of touch and leaving Lee unapprised of what force he was facing, and the lateness of Longstreet's attack on the second day—either wasn't a blunder at all (if Longstreet had attacked earlier he would have encountered an even stronger Union position) or was caused by a lack of forcefulness and specificity in Lee's orders.

Before Gettysburg, Lee had seemed not only to read the minds of Union generals but almost to expect his subordinates to read his. He was not in fact good at telling men what to do. That no doubt suited the Confederate fighting man, who didn't take kindly to being told what to do—but Lee's only weakness as a commander, his otherwise reverent nephew Fitzhugh Lee would write, was his "reluctance to oppose the wishes of others, or to order them to do anything that would be disagreeable and to which they would not consent." With men as well as with women, his authority derived from his sightliness, politeness, and unimpeachability. His usually cheerful detachment patently covered solemn depths, depths faintly lit by glints of previous and potential rejection of self and others. It all seemed Olympian, in a Christian cavalier sort of way. Officers' hearts went out to him across the latitude he granted them to be willingly, creatively honorable. Longstreet speaks of responding to Lee at another critical moment by "receiving his anxious expressions really as appeals for reinforcement of his unexpressed wish." When people obey you because they think you enable them to follow their own instincts, you need a keen instinct yourself for when they're getting out of touch, as Stuart did, and when they are balking for good reason, as Longstreet did. As a father Lee was fond but fretful, as a husband devoted but distant, as a slave master unvicious but feckless. As an attacking general he was inspiring but not necessarily cogent.

At Gettysburg he was jittery, snappish. He was fifty-six and bone weary. He may have had dysentery, though a scholar's widely publicized assertion to that effect rests on tenuous evidence. He did have rheumatism and heart trouble. He kept fretfully wondering why Stuart was out of touch, worrying that something bad had happened to him. He had given Stuart broad discretion as usual, and Stuart, perhaps out to make people forget Brandy Station, had overextended himself. Stuart wasn't frolicking. He had done his best to act on Lee's written instructions: "You will . . . be able to judge whether you can pass around their army without hinderance, doing them all the damage you can, and cross the [Potomac] east of the mountains. In either case, after crossing the river, you must move on and feel the right of Ewell's troops, collecting information, provisions, etc." But he had not, in fact, been able to judge: He met several hindrances in the form of Union troops, a swollen river that he and his men managed only heroically to cross, and 150 Federal wagons that he captured *before* he crossed the river. And he had not sent word of what he was up to.

When on the afternoon of the second day Stuart did show up at Gettysburg, after pushing himself nearly to exhaustion, Lee's only greeting to him is said to have been, "Well, General Stuart, you are here at last." A coolly devastating cut: Lee's way of chewing out someone who he felt had let him down. In the months after Gettysburg, as Lee stewed over his defeat, he repeatedly criticized the laxness of Stuart's command, deeply hurting a man who prided himself on the sort of dashing freelance effectiveness by which Light-Horse Harry had defined himself. A bond of implicit trust had been broken. Loving-son figure had failed loving-father figure and vice versa.

In the past Lee had also granted Ewell and Longstreet wide discretion, and it had paid off. Maybe his magic in Virginia didn't travel. "The whole affair was disjointed," Taylor the aide said of Gettysburg. "There was an utter absence of accord in the movements of the several commands."

Why did Lee stake everything, finally, on an ill-considered thrust straight up the middle?

Lee's critics have never come up with a logical explanation. Evidently he just got his blood up, as the expression goes. When the usually repressed Lee felt an overpowering need for emotional release, and had an army at his disposal and another one in front of him, he couldn't hold back. And why should Lee expect his imprudence to be any less unsettling to Meade than it had been to the other Union commanders?

The spot against which he hurled Pickett was right in front of Meade's headquarters. Once Dwight Eisenhower, who admired Lee's generalship, took Field Marshal Montgomery to visit the Gettysburg battlefield. They looked at the site of Pickett's charge and were baffled. Eisenhower said, "The man [Lee] must have got so mad that he wanted to hit that guy [Meade] with a brick." But when Meade came to the breastworks in person, he found to his surprise that Pickett had already been repulsed. Only then did he succumb to Leephobia, by failing to order a counterattack that might have destroyed Lee's army.

In an essay published in a collection entitled *The Gettysburg Nobody Knows,* historian Kent Gramm accounts for Gettysburg in terms of chaos theory. Positing chaos as a principle of order may be no more than a fast shuffle, but if you can believe, with chaos theorists, that the fluttering of a butterfly wing can eventually result in a tornado thousands of miles away—well, in fact, if Pickett's charge had not been met as redoubtably as it was, the Federal line might have broken. Meanwhile Stuart was trying to come at that line from the left: his cavalry engaging Gen. George Custer's in one last old-fashioned saber-waving cavalry clash. A Union officer described it: "As the two columns approached each other the pace of each increased, when suddenly a crash, like the falling of timber, betokened the crisis. So sudden and violent was the collision that many of the horses were turned end over end and crushed their riders beneath them." It was a standoff, but if Stuart had won, he could have come into the rear of the position Pickett was attacking.

And Lee would have prevailed miraculously again, and the North would have been demoralized, and Americans would have to go through customs now in the Atlanta airport.

If you can believe that, how about this:

Meade's headquarters was a thousand yards or so from the Baltimore Pike. Lee's was about the same distance from the Mummasburg Road. When Light-Horse Harry Lee was just about Lee's age at Gettysburg, he came to grief in Baltimore. It was a man known to history only as "a giant of a man named Mumma" who tried to cut off his nose.

Maybe something in Harry's son decided, *this is the place*. To win his war or lose it, to resolve his oedipal conflict or not. It was no place, certainly, where he was about to be swayed by Longstreet's defensive instincts and run the risk of being trapped. Maybe Lee saw "those people" as the mob that savaged his father, the man who believed in "We, the people" until he saw what that could come to. So the aging Robert flung his Miserables against Cemetery Ridge in a kind of adolescent ecstasy.

Pickett's troops, at any rate, advanced with precision, closed up the gaps that withering fire tore into their smartly dressed ranks, and at close quarters fought tooth and nail. A couple of hundred Confederates did break the Union line, but only briefly. Someone counted fifteen bodies on a patch of ground that measured less than five feet wide and three feet long. It has been estimated that 10,500 Johnny Rebs made the charge and 5,675—roughly 54 percent—fell dead or wounded. As a Captain Spessard charged, he saw his son shot dead. He laid him out gently on the ground, kissed him, and got back to advancing.

As the minority who hadn't been cut to ribbons streamed back to the Confederate lines, Lee rode in splendid calm among them, apologizing. "It's all my fault," he assured stunned privates and corporals. He took the time to admonish, mildly, an officer who was beating his horse: "Don't whip him, captain; it does no good. I had a foolish horse, once, and kind treatment is the best." Then he resumed his apologies: "I am very sorry—the task was too great for you— but we mustn't despond." Shelby Foote has called this Lee's finest moment. But generals don't want apologies from those beneath them, and that goes both ways.

After midnight that night, he told a cavalry officer, "I never saw troops behave more magnificently than Pickett's division of Virginians. . . ." Then he fell silent, and it was then that he exclaimed, as the officer later wrote it down, "Too bad! *Too bad!* OH! TOO BAD!"

Pickett's charge wasn't the half of it. Altogether at Gettysburg as many as 28,000 Confederates were killed, wounded, captured, or missing: more than a third of Lee's whole army. Perhaps it was because Meade and his troops were so stunned by their own losses—about 20,000—that they failed to pursue Lee on his withdrawal south, trap him against the flooded Potomac, and wipe his army out. Lincoln and the Northern press were furious that this didn't happen.

For months Lee had been traveling with a pet hen. Meant for the stewpot, she had won his heart by entering his tent first thing every morning (after pacing back and forth in front of the entrance for a while to get the timing just right) and laying his breakfast egg under his Spartan cot. As the Army of Northern Virginia was breaking camp in all deliberate speed for the withdrawal, Lee's staff ran around anxiously crying, *"Where is the hen?"* Lee himself found her nestled in her accustomed spot on the wagon that transported his personal matériel. Life goes on.

On July 4, 1863, the day after Gettysburg, Vicksburg surrendered to Grant. Grant headed east, toward Lee, who retreated back to Virginia and offered Jefferson Davis his resignation, but Davis refused it. Both of them were determined not to let Richmond suffer Vicksburg's fate.

The ruling class of Richmond was keeping up its spirits by clinging to its anachronistic affinity for high romance. During the winter (off-season for warfare) after Gettysburg, the Richmond smart crowd tossed a grand party culminating in a series of charades. The grandest charade enacted the word *pilgrimage.* First someone pretending to take a *pill,* then someone looking *grim,* then someone showing *age,* and then the whole word. According to an account unearthed by Emory Thomas, "[T]he stage became a shrine, draped and flower strewn, the Cross surmounting it. Toward it slowly moved pilgrims. . . . Peasant, priest, Knight . . . kneeling to lay their offerings upon the Cross. . . . The band struck up 'See! The conquering hero comes.' Forth strode grand 'Jeb' Stuart, in full uniform, his stainless sword unsheathed, his noble face luminous with inward fire." Stuart, for it was he in the role of himself (if he'd been a private, attending this party would have been straggling), advanced, laid his sword on the shrine "as votive offering," and stepped back, his arms folded, his eyes down. Socialites in nuns' habits blessed the sword. Others dressed as Muslims touched it and fell prostrate. "The music had softened to a sweet pianissimo as the sword was laid upon the altar. Now it swelled out into a solemn strain, and the Franciscans, the Paulists, the Capuchins and the nuns in the pilgrimages stood forth and chanted the 'Miserere,' as the refrain softly closed."

High-church folderol. That's what the junior officers denounced, who got so exercised over Puseyism during that argument back before the war. *"Beware of Pussyism!"* Lee had jokingly advised them. "Beware of votive offerings," he might have said in deep seriousness to the Southerners among them.

On November 19 Lincoln spoke at the dedication of a cemetery in Gettysburg, where most of the Union dead from that battle were buried. He called upon all those present at the ceremony to "resolve that these dead shall not have died in vain—that this nation, under God, shall have a new birth of freedom—and that government of the people, by the people, for the people shall not perish from the earth."

During the winter Lee took time only for brief visits with his wife, whose physical deterioration was marked. "I see . . . you are relapsing into your old error," he had written her, "that I have a superabundance of time & have only my own pleasures to attend to." Rooney was a prisoner of war. Rooney's wife, Chass, on whom Robert doted, died after a long illness. Young Rob was serving under his cousin Fitzhugh. Custis was looking after his mother—the surviving daughters were with her, too—and doing staff duty in Richmond. Lee had not been with his family for Christmas since 1859. He spent this one, too, with his troops.

Hostilities began again in the spring of 1864.

Lee never mounted another murderous head-on assault. He went on the defensive. Grant took over command of the eastern front and 118,700 men. He set out to grind Lee's 64,000 down. Lee had his men well dug in. Grant resolved to turn his flank, force him into a weaker position, and crush him.

In retrospect Lee was prolonging the agony beyond all reason. He was defending his home state to the last ditch, and in the process helping to turn it into one barren, bloody ditch after another. But he was a soldier, and his government refused to surrender—or to support him adequately. At one point he went to the Confederate Congress to plead that they do more to supply his troops. "Well, Mr. Custis," he reported to his son, "I have been up to see the Congress and they do not seem to be able to do anything except eat peanuts and chew tobacco, while my army is starving. . . . Mr. Custis, when this war began, I was opposed to it, bitterly opposed to it, and I told these people that, unless every man should do his whole duty, they would repent it; and now . . . they will repent." Light-Horse Harry would have lit into "these people" publicly, early and late, but look what happened to him.

If Robert could get nowhere with the politicians, he was determined not to let Grant lick him. For the record at least he didn't speak of the Union commander in personal terms, except when a Federal courier requesting a cease-fire for burial of the dead conveyed to him Grant's message, "Give General Lee my personal compliments, and say to him that I keep such close touch with him that I know what he eats for breakfast every morning." Lee's reply was to "tell General Grant that . . . unless he had fallen from grace since I last saw him, he would not permit me to eat such a breakfast as mine without dividing his with me. I also requested that officer to present my compliments to General Grant, and say to him that I knew perhaps as much about his dinners as he knew about my breakfasts."

But he knew he was dealing now with an opponent who would not back off or split any differences. "Ulysses don't scare worth a damn," said one of Grant's men. Grant did not rely, as Lee so often did, on intuition. Whereas Lee with his antennae was courtly and deferential toward Jefferson Davis, Grant spoke up to Lincoln, and Lincoln respected him for it. Grant was not inclined to fall philosophically back into the arms of God. He didn't like face-to-face arguments, but he could firmly and clearly tell subordinates what to do, and he was a strict disciplinarian. He conquered his own bad drinking habit, and when he found one of his men drunk he knocked him down, tied him up and gagged him, and had him thrown into the guardhouse. When one of his officers spoke apprehensively of what Lee might be up to, Grant stood up, took his cigar out of his mouth, and said, "Oh, I am heartily tired of hearing about what *Lee* is going to do. Some of you always seem to think he is suddenly going to turn a double somersault, and land in our rear and on both of our flanks at the same time. Go back to your command, and try to think what we are going to do ourselves, instead of what *Lee* is going to do."

Grant had a chip on his shoulder, because, when he was winning victories in the west, "It was not an uncommon thing for my staff-officers to hear from Eastern officers, 'Well, Grant has never met Bobby Lee yet.'" According to Charles A. Dana, who was sent by Secretary of War Edwin Stanton to report back from Grant's headquarters, Grant admired Lee's tactics on defense, but not on offense—he felt that Lee's bold strokes at Chancellorsville had been reckless. After the war, Grant still resented the acclaim that Lee got: "I never ranked Lee so high as some others in the army; that is to say I never had so much anxiety when he was in my front as when Joe Johnston was at my front. Lee was a good man, a fair commander, and had everything in his favour. . . . Lee was of a slow, cautious nature, without imagination, or humour, always the same, with grave dignity." This was not a very perceptive analysis (by "everything in his favour," Grant seemed to mean that Lee got such a good press), but it no doubt kept Grant's confidence up. He kept pressing. The Confederates inflicted considerably more casualties than they sustained, but the Federals had many more bodies to spare.

By now most of Lee's surviving officers were nonprofessional, so he was far more closely involved in tactics than before, and his defensive maneuvers and positioning in 1864 and 1865 were brilliant. The old engineer advanced the art of entrenchment, and the Virginian who as a boy would beat the foxhunters to the fox on foot kept repositioning himself between Grant and Richmond. Inexorably, however, Grant gained ground.

Lee was just delaying the inevitable now, at the cost of thousands and thousands more lives. He was sick, often irascible. In action he was inspirational but sometimes almost crazed. During the insanely sanguinary fighting in the Wilderness (the same almost impassable terrain that Jackson had slipped through to pull off the coup at Chancellorsville), Lee had to be restrained four times from wading into the thick of horrific bloodshed. Once, recalled Gen. John Gordon, Lee with head bared and looking like "a very god of war" rode "calmly and grandly . . . to the point near the center of my line and turned his horse's head to the front, evidently resolved to lead in person the desperate charge and drive [the Union] back or perish in the effort." Gordon grabbed Traveller's bridle and said, "These men . . . have never failed you on any field. They will not fail you here. Will you boys?"

"No!" the boys cried. "Lee to the rear! Lee to the rear!" He acceded, and the boys charged with a vengeance. Another time, after Traveller's sudden rearing prevented him from being struck by a projectile that passed directly under the horse's girth (making up for the time he'd caused his master to break his hands), Lee cried, "Hurrah for Texas!" and jumped into the lead of an advancing column of Texans. "Go back, General, go back!" the men cried. "I wish I knew where my place is on the battlefield," Lee grumbled. "Wherever I go someone tells me that is not the place to be!" Once he mused that it would be a relief to ride along in full view of sharp-shooters and get put out of his misery, and many of his soldiers may have had the same feeling. The following anecdote from Freeman's biography seems evidence not so much of gallantry as of collective insanity:

> "Orendorf," said Colonel Christian to a tall, thin boy from Amherst County, "will you carry the colors?"
>
> "Yes, Colonel," Orendorf answered, "I will carry them. They killed my brother the other day; now, damn them, let them kill me." . . .
>
> Orendorf was torn to bits by a cannon ball, as he defiantly waved his flag not twenty feet from the enemy.

On the battlefields of the Wilderness and around Spotsylvania, Confederate ordnance men picked up more than 120,000 ounces of lead for recasting, which led Gen. J. F. C. Fuller to estimate, on the assumption that they probably found only a twentieth of the bullets that had been fired there, that the total number was nineteen million. A tree twenty-two inches in diameter was cut through by bullets as if a beaver had gnawed it down.

The battlefield of the Wilderness was thick piney woods, which caught fire from the shelling. Many wounded men burned to death. Even some of the log-and-sod breastworks caught fire. Confederate riflemen stayed there, firing through the flames.

In a skirmish against Gen. Phil Sheridan's cavalry, which was threatening Richmond at a place just north of there called Yellow Tavern, Stuart took a pistol bullet in the gut. "Honey-bun, how do I look in the face?" he asked an officer named Hullihen. He traveled in one of those jouncing ambulances to Richmond, reluctantly consented to take a bit of medicinal whiskey despite his vow to his mother, and said, "I am resigned if it be God's will but I would like to see my wife." Flora and the children were coming as fast as they could, but a bridge was out, and they were stopped on Richmond's outskirts by a Confederate picket who actually tried to shoot them, but his gun misfired. By the time she reached Beauty, he had succumbed with his boots off after twenty-six hours of intestinal agony. On hearing that Stuart was mortally wounded, Lee said in a voice full of emotion, "He never brought me a piece of false information." On hearing that Stuart was dead: "I can scarcely think of him without weeping." But Lee wrote a note to himself: "The warmest instincts of every man's soul declare the glory of the soldier's death."

Perhaps the least gallant episode of the war's denouement was at Cold Harbor in 1864. Grant got frustrated and resorted to one of those Napoleonic murder charges against Lee's well-built fortification. Something like seven thousand Union soldiers were mowed down in a matter of minutes. One Yankee, Robert Stiles recalled, somehow managed to reach the Confederate line. He "bounded over the work and landed right in among us; but he ran on toward the rear and brought up in a sitting posture on a pile of earth one of the infantry had thrown out of a hole he had dug to cook in. . . . The man's back was turned toward us, his elbows were on his knees, and his head sunk in his hands." Then one of Stiles's men was hit and cried, "Oh God, I'm done forever." After easing this man's last moments during a lull in the onslaught, Stiles noticed that the Union man was still sitting on the kitchen heap. Assuming him to be wounded, he sent one of his men to bring him to a spot less exposed to his own side's fire, "but he cast off our hands and we had to leave him to his fate. In a few minutes he was shot in the head and tumbled in upon the cook in the kitchen—dead." The charge took its toll on Lee's army: some fifteen hundred Confederate casualties in the same brief span of time, including fifteen-year-old John Christian, who'd been at war for six weeks. "Poor boy," wrote a fellow private, "a shell took off his head while he was bravely doing his duty like an old vet." But the assault broke down into heaps of Union flesh. It was Lee's last big victory, and as one-sided as Fredericksburg. Years later Grant would cite the decision to attack Cold Harbor as a regrettable mistake. But neither he nor Lee seems to have acknowledged how callously they behaved over the next few days.

Grant didn't want to admit defeat, so he requested permission to gather up his wounded without flying the customary white flag, which would protect his litter bearers from Confederate sharpshooters. Lee wasn't having it. "I fear that such an arrangement will lead to misunderstanding and difficulty," he responded. Grant sat down and wrote an affectionate letter to his daughter, Nellie, promising her a present for her ninth birthday: a buggy for her pony to pull. For four days, while messages regarding protocol went back and forth, thousands of Union wounded lay roasting and piteously "mewling" (as Shelby Foote puts it) in the heat of the sun. Among the Union officers at Cold Harbor was Oliver Wendell Holmes Jr., who would go on to become the great humanist justice of the U.S. Supreme Court. "It's odd," Holmes had written months before to his father, the renowned whimsical author, "how indifferent one gets to the sight of death—perhaps, because one gets aristocratic and don't value much a common life. Then they are apt to be so dirty it seems natural—'Dust to Dust.'" By the time Grant finally agreed to fly the flag of truce, only two of the wounded men were still alive.

Many of the Cold Harbor dead were buried in Mary Lee's front yard. That spring George Meigs, an angry Georgian who had served under Lee before the war but had remained with the Union and become quartermaster general, had turned her old homeplace into a national cemetery. Those people.

Lee hoped to hold Grant off long enough to influence the U.S. presidential election in favor of the peace-seeking Democrats, who nominated McClellan to oppose Lincoln, but Atlanta fell and so, once again, did McClellan. And so, finally, did Richmond.

If Grant ever got them besieged, Lee had said, it was over. They were besieged, at Petersburg. They dug in and kept fighting. Union soldiers came upon A. P. Hill after piercing his lines. He tried to bluff them into surrendering to him. They shot him through the heart. When Lee heard, he burst into tears and said, "He is now at rest, and we who are left are the ones to suffer." Lee sent Jubal Early's division into the Shenandoah Valley. They won victories against Sheridan and even got close enough to Washington for Lincoln to come out on a balcony and see them coming, but Grant sent reinforcements, the threat to Washington subsided, and soon Early's force was crushed.

At one point, according to one of his early biographers,

Lee lingered under artillery fire to pick up a fallen baby bird and restore it to its nest.

They ate the pet hen.

When Lincoln was reelected, in November 1864, ending Southern hopes that a Democratic administration in Washington would negotiate a peace, Lee wrote to his wife, "We must therefore make up our minds for another four years of war."

In January 1865 Confederate troops were angered to encounter black troops, including escaped slaves, and in more than one incident they slaughtered black soldiers who were trying to surrender. Lee is not known to have made any comment on this. He did propose the enlistment of slaves into his army in return for the emancipation of them and (at the end of the war) their families, along with "a well-digested plan of gradual and general emancipation." His reasoning, no doubt pitched to the prejudices of the Confederate Congress:

> Considering the relation of master and slave, controlled by humane laws and influenced by Christianity and an enlightened public sentiment, as the best that can exist between the white and black races while intermingled as at present in this country, I would deprecate any sudden disturbance of that relation unless it be necessary to avert a greater calamity to both. Whatever may be the effect of our employing negro troops, it cannot be as mischievous as this. If it end in subverting slavery it will be accomplished by ourselves, and we can devise the means of alleviating the

evil consequences to both races. I think, therefore, we must decide whether slavery shall be extinguished by our enemies and the slaves be used against us, or use them ourselves at the risk of the effects which may be produced upon our social institutions. My own opinion is that we should employ them without delay.

The Confederate Congress on March 13, 1865, voted reluctantly and narrowly to enlist slave soldiers, adding, "Nothing in this act shall be construed to authorize a change in the relation which said slaves shall bear toward their owners, except by consent of the owners and of the States in which they may reside."

The best comment on this absurd bit of race relations was a cartoon in *Harper's Weekly* that showed a "Chivalric Southerner" saying, "Here! You mean, inferior, degraded Chattel, jest kitch holt of one of them 'ere muskets, and *conquer my freedom for me!*" and the "Chattel" responding, "Well, dunno, Massa; guess you'd better not be free: you know, Massa, *slave folks is a deal happier than free folks.*"

What was left of Lee's army still had spirit. Custer confronted Longstreet and said, "[U]nless you surrender immediately we are going to pitch in."

"Pitch in as much as you like," said Longstreet.

But if that one last battle had erupted, it would have been murder indeed. On April 9, 1865, Lee finally had to admit that he was trapped. At the beginning of Lee's long, combative retreat by stages from Grant's overpowering numbers, he had 64,000 men. By the end they had inflicted 63,000 Union casualties but had been reduced themselves to fewer than 10,000, perhaps less than two thirds of whom had any arms left to stack.

To be sure, there were those in Lee's army who proposed continuing the struggle as guerrillas or by reorganizing under the governors of the various Confederate states. "We would be like rabbits and partridges in the bushes, and [Grant's troops] could not scatter to follow us," argued Col. Edward Porter Alexander, his artillery commander.

Lee cut off any such talk. He was a professional soldier. He had seen more than enough of governors who would be commanders, and he had no respect for ragtag guerrilladom. "If I took your advice," he told Porter, "the men . . . would become mere bands of marauders, and the enemy's cavalry would pursue them and overrun many wide sections they may never have occasion to visit. We would bring on a state of affairs it would take the country years to recover from.

"And, as for myself, you young fellows might go to bush-whacking, but the only dignified course for me would be, to go to Gen. Grant and surrender myself and take the consequences."

Though in the field Lee had carried no weapon and worn no insignia of rank, to meet with Grant at a farmhouse in the village of Appomattox Court House he put on a full-dress uniform and borrowed a ceremonial sword (which he did not surrender). Grant arrived from the field looking perhaps pointedly scruffy.

The occasion was solemn, and gracious on both sides. Grant had told his generals he "had no doubt about the good faith of Lee." At Lee's request Grant readily agreed to send food to Lee's men, many of whom had been without rations for a week, and to allow those who still had horses or mules to ride them home. (The rations Grant turned over had been seized by Sheridan's troops from a supply train on its way to Lee.)

Lee emerged from the house, called, "Orderly!" and Taylor brought him Traveller. He rode away. Grant came out. Everyone wondered what statement he would make. He turned to one of his generals and said, "Ingalls, do you remember that old white mule that so-and-so used to ride when we were in the city of Mexico?" That was it. Had Lee reminded him of that old mule? Surely not. Maybe Grant felt as tired as that old mule.

A young Boston Brahmin aide to General Meade was introduced to Lee: "a stately-looking man, tall, erect and strongly built, with a full chest . . . He has a large and well-shaped head, with a brown, clear eye, of unusual depth. . . . [H]e is exceedingly grave and dignified . . . but there was evidently added an extreme depression, which gave him the air of a man who kept up his pride to the last, but who was entirely overwhelmed. From his speech I judge he was inclined to wander in his thoughts. . . . Lee put out his hand and saluted us with all the air of the oldest blood in the world."

Lee's troops were eating, at last, when he rejoined them. They cheered him. No orator, he mumbled a few words—according to Robert Jr., "Men, we have fought through the war together; I have done my best for you; my heart is too full to say more"—and assigned a staff officer to write, to his specifications, his eloquent farewell address, which was read out to what was left of his men by what was left of their unit commanders:

> After four years of arduous service, marked by unsurpassed courage and fortitude, the Army of Northern Virginia has been compelled to yield to overwhelming numbers and resources. I need not tell the survivors of so many hard-fought battles, who have remained steadfast to the last, that I have consented to this result from no distrust of them, but, feeling that valor and devotion could accomplish nothing that could compensate for the loss that would have attended the continuation of the contest, I have determined to avoid the useless sacrifice of those whose past services have endeared them to their countrymen.
>
> By the terms of the agreement, officers and men can return to their homes, and remain there until exchanged. You will take with you the satisfaction that proceeds from the consciousness of duty faithfully performed; and I earnestly pray that a merciful God will extend to you his blessing and protection.
>
> With an increasing admiration of your constancy and devotion to your country, and a grateful remembrance of your kind and generous consideration of myself, I bid you an affectionate farewell.
>
> R. E. Lee, General

Lee struck out another paragraph because he felt it "would tend to keep alive the feeling existing between North and South." On April 20 Lee reported to Jefferson Davis that 7,892 infantry had surrendered with him, and then the stragglers had started coming in. Within three days the number of surrendering ex-soldiers of the Army of Northern Virginia had grown to 26,018, and many more showed up in Richmond over the next few days. "I have given these details," Lee wrote to Davis, "that your Excellency might know the state of feeling which existed in the army, and judge of that in the country." The feeling had been of despair. Far more troops rallied to weary surrender than had been showing up for grisly duty.

CHAPTER NINE

THOMAS MORRIS CHESTER, the only black correspondent for a major daily (the *Philadelphia Press*) during the war, had nothing but scorn for the Confederacy, and referred to Lee as a "notorious rebel," whom Grant had caused "the most unpleasant anxiety of his unnatural life." But when Chester witnessed Lee's arrival in shattered, burned-out Richmond after the surrender, he was moved to write:

> The general with affable dignity received the marks of respect which were manifested by those who happened along the pavement. Several efforts were made to cheer him, which failed, until within a short distance of his residence, previous to which his admirers satisfied themselves with quietly waving their hats and their hands. . . . At his mansion, on Franklin street, where he alighted from his horse, he immediately uncovered his head, thinly covered with silver hairs, as he had done in acknowledgment of the veneration of the people along the streets. There was a general rush of the small crowd to shake hands with him.
>
> During these manifestations not a word was spoken, and when the ceremony was through, the General bowed and

ascended his steps. The silence was then broken by a few voices calling for a speech, to which he paid no attention. The General then passed into his house, and the crowd dispersed.

But it was not his mansion, it was the one lent to Mary by friends. Charles A. Dana wrote that Grant told him that in his "long private interview" with Lee at Appomattox, Lee had said he was left by the war "a poor man, with nothing but what he had upon his person, and his wife would have to provide for herself until he could find some employment." It seems hardly likely that Lee would confide to Grant, of all people, about his finances, but if he didn't say it he was undoubtedly thinking it. Lee was even poorer now than in his boyhood, when his father left home. And in the outrage that followed Lincoln's assassination, he was indicted for treason. Grant interceded with Andrew Johnson and wrote to Lee that he needn't worry about being tried, but the indictment was not dropped formally until 1869. When Lee signed and submitted an amnesty oath (common folk in the South called this "swallowing the dog") shortly after Appomattox, he was not accorded the courtesy of a response. Secretary of State William H. Seward gave the document to a friend of his for a souvenir. Lee would not be not granted full citizenship until 1975, by President Gerald Ford.

Lee was offered lucrative employment—figurehead of an insurance company, for instance. "General Lee says: 'Southern Prudential has your loved ones' security at heart'"? No. What he did, in the last five years of his life, was serve as a much better president of a small, impoverished college than

Grant of the United States in the Gilded Age. And although shortly after Grant was inaugurated Lee wrote to a young cousin, "Our boasted self Govt. is fast becoming the jeer & laughing stock of the world," publicly he urged Southerners to obey the Federal laws of Reconstruction—to reconcile themselves to the government of those people, by those people, and for those people. For a while he was vilified in the Northern press, but gradually his bent for mediation came to be regarded as a national asset, even though—or because—he continued to believe firmly if not demonstratively that white conservatives should be in control. We may assume that, had he lived to see it, Lee—along with a vast majority of white Americans North and South—would have been in accord with the abandonment, in 1876, of the federally imposed effort to advance black people's opportunities in the South.

But there is a story, printed in the *Confederate Veteran* in 1905 and accepted by Emory Thomas, that Lee, shortly after the surrender, took at least one step toward racial integration. At Saint Paul's Church in Richmond, when the rector invited the congregation to come forward and take Communion, a well-dressed very black man was the first to respond. To anyone who grew up in the segregated South before the Civil Rights Act of 1964, it is amazing that this man was even allowed to attend the service, but this was in 1865, before the Jim Crow laws that came in after 1876. Before the war, mixed congregations in Virginia were apparently not unheard of. The Lexington Presbyterian Church, which Stonewall Jackson attended, had 307 white and 11 black members. That day in Saint Paul's, however, the black man's action seemed to be an effort to embarrass, and no one came forward to join him at the altar until Lee arose from his pew, strode to the chancel rail, and knelt. The rest of the distinguished congregation followed suit.

Called before the congressional Reconstruction committee, Lee managed coolly to avoid giving Republicans anything regarded, at the time, as red meat. Asked whether, in the case of war with a foreign power, he would favor Virginia's seceding again and siding with the enemy, he said, "I have no disposition now to do it, and I never have had." Asked how Virginians regarded the North now, he said, "They think that the North can afford to be generous." Asked whether he thought that Virginia would be better off if "the colored population" went to other Southern states, he said, "I think it would be better for Virginia if she could get rid of them. . . . I have always thought so, and have always been in favor of emancipation—gradual emancipation." Probed further, he said that blacks "are an amiable, social race. They like their ease and comfort, and, I think, look more to the present time than to the future." He did not think that "at this time" they could "vote intelligently." He also didn't think them "as capable of acquiring knowledge as the white man is. Some are more apt than others."

These were pretty much the genteel opinions of the time, North and South. (Grant in his memoirs wrote that to save the Republican Party after the war "it became necessary to enfranchise the negro, in all his ignorance.") Mary Lee was more outspoken: "I would think soon all *decent white* people would be forced to retire from [Washington] and give place to the dominant race." Lee's racial attitudes did not interfere with his work as an educator, because Washington College in Lexington, Virginia, was a private school for white men, in which context he was able to tell a faculty member, "Always observe the stage driver's rule. Always take care of the *poor* horses"–look after the weaker students, who needed help. His starting salary at the college, which had been sacked by Union troops in the last year of the war and which had only twenty-five students when he assumed the presidency, was only $1,500, but a pleasant house was built for him, with state-of-the-art plumbing and heating and a wraparound porch on three sides. And in the second year of his tenure, a 100 percent raise and his 20 percent cut of each student's $75 tuition brought his compensation to $4,756, a good upper-middle-class living.

He modernized the curriculum to include postclassical literature, modern languages, law, even journalism. He attended chapel every day but ended compulsory attendance for students. He said of a student who was not applying himself, "He is a very quiet, orderly young man, but seems very careful not to injure the health of his father's son. Now, I do not want our young men really to injure their health, but I wish them to come as near to it as possible." But when another student who was in fact endangering his health by over-work explained that he was "impatient to make up for the time I lost in the army," Lee got red in the face and expostulated: "Mister Humphreys! However long you live and whatever you accomplish, you will find that the time you spent in the Confederate army was the most profitably spent portion of your life." In his heart of hearts Lee had reason to share this student's feelings, but he was damned if he'd admit it, even perhaps to himself. Lee himself, however, expressly put soldiering behind him. When his students and those of the Virginia Military Institute marched together, Lee, walking along with VMI's commandant, made a point of marching out of step. Except in his days as a West Point cadet, when he'd obeyed the rules so assiduously as to set himself apart, and perhaps in Mexico, where he had extended himself brilliantly for the exhilaration of it and for General Scott's fatherly, affectionate approval, he had never been in step with military convention—as a commander, his anomalousness had been his strength. Now he was free literally to march to a different drummer.

The rapidly expanding student body regarded him with awe and found him aloof. "He seemed to avoid contact with men," said one. He gave them only one day for Christmas vacation, and threatened to kick them all out of school when they petitioned for a week. He rode in the mountains on Traveller, often with Mildred, and he enjoyed the company of the faculty's and neighbors' little daughters. A shy one who had been afraid to approach him finally tiptoed to his bedroom door, saw a penwiper shaped like a man, and asked, "Is that your doll-baby?"

"Yes," said Lee, and the little girl came in for a chat.

He enjoyed hearing about courtly attentions. Of a young man who was paying frequent visits to a family houseguest, a Miss Long, Lee remarked: "He wants but little here below, but he wants that little Long."

Traveller had the run of the lawn, even when he browsed on the shrubbery. There were cats and a dog and Mildred's pet hens, which she named after herself and friends. It is not hard to imagine Lee coming upon one of these chickens and saying, "Good morning, Laura Chilton."

At the White Sulphur Springs resort, where he went for the mineral baths, he attended a dance where some Northern guests were being ostracized. He induced some of the Southern young ladies to join him in breaking the ice with the Yankees. "But, General Lee, did you never feel resentment toward the North?" asked one of the belles. And according to her recollection, "Standing in the radiance of the myriad lighted crystals his face took on a far-away, almost inspired look, as his hand involuntarily sought his breast. He spoke in low, earnest tones. 'I believe I may say, looking into my heart, and speaking as in the presence of my God, that I have never known one moment of bitterness or resentment.'" Ritualistic denial, no doubt, but suitable to the setting, and greatly to be preferred, as we have seen since in other parts of the world, to religious vengefulness.

And he intervened, twice, to avert the sort of mob violence that had broken his father. The younger brother of two of his students had been shot in the course of a fight with a young black man named Caesar Griffin. Students captured Griffin, put a rope around his neck, and would not be calmed by teachers from the college. Suddenly the raging crowd hushed: Lee had arrived. "Young gentlemen," he said calmly, "let the law take its course." They turned over the prisoner to town officials. Then, when rumors spread that the white youth was dying and there was talk of storming the jail, Lee acted behind the scenes to quash any such sentiment. The wounded youth recovered, and Griffin went before a circuit judge who sent him to prison for two years. This was Reconstruction Virginia under military rule and the glare of the Northern press (the *Chicago Tribune* had charged that Washington College was "run principally for the propagation of hatred to the Union"), but due process prevailed under local authorities, and the college's reputation survived, thanks in large part to a word here and there from Lee.

Lee made some effort to write his memoirs of the war, but so many Confederate records had been destroyed, his health was far from robust, and he had little free time. He did edit a new edition of Light-Horse Harry's memoir of the Revolution. His introduction to that book, a stilted biographical sketch that mentioned none of his father's failings or humiliations, is the only thing he ever wrote for publication. He assigned the proceeds to his oldest brother, Carter, who had received all of Harry's paternal letters and hadn't amounted to much.

In May 1869, at Grant's invitation, Lee paid him a visit in the White House. It was brief. Neither man left an account of it. They had little, certainly nothing personal or political, to say to each other. "All that Grant could remember afterwards," said an aide, "was that they spoke of building railroads, and he said playfully to Lee, 'You and I, General, have had more to do with destroying railroads than building them.' But Lee refused to smile, or to recognize the raillery." The matter was no playful one in the desperately war-blighted South, which had had few enough rails to begin with, most of which had been ripped up and wrapped around trees by Federal troops. And Grant might have had the sensitivity to bear in mind that Lee, shortly after taking over the Army of Northern Virginia, had been the first general in history to mobilize artillery by mounting it on railroad cars.

That summer, just as Lee had settled Mary into one spa and was looking forward to resting his bones at another, he received word that his older brother Smith Lee, whose white teeth had shone so cheerfully through the smoke of battle in Mexico, had died at his farm near Alexandria. Robert, arriving too late for the funeral, wrote to Mary, "May God . . . preserve us for the time when we, too, must part, the one from the other, which is now close at hand." Smith had served out the war in Richmond as an administrative admiral in the Confederate navy, whose force comprised a surplus of former senior U.S. Navy officers and scarcely any seapower. In history Smith left no mark whatever aside from the not inconsiderable one of appealing more than Robert did to Mary Chesnut. Robert and Smith "had always kept warm their boyish love," a relative wrote. "It was delightful to see them together and listen to their stories of the happy long ago they would tell about each other."

Robert visited Fitzhugh, Smith's son, at that branch of the family's estate, Ravensworth, where the unpropertied Ann Carter Lee had gone to die. Robert wrote to his wife, "Forty years ago I stood in this room by my mother's deathbed! It seems now but yesterday!"

"You know she is like her papa—always wanting something," Lee said of his daughter Agnes. Lee's children often seemed to find themselves wanting, in complicated ways. Agnes, for instance, wrote in an adolescent journal, "I do wish I was a Christian! But it is so hard to be one. I am afraid I don't feel that I need a Saviour as deeply as I ought." Maybe that's how you feel when you have a martyr for a papa.

"Having distributed such poor Christmas gifts as I had around me, I have been looking for something for you," Lee wrote to his big-nosed, abidingly disgruntled daughter Mary on the first December 25 of the Civil War. "I send you some sweet violets that I gathered for you this morning while covered with dense white frost, whose crystals glittered in the bright sun like diamonds." Generally, Lee was careful with his syntax, but here he seems to cover himself, gloriously, with dense frost. What had he been looking for, himself?

What he had been given was the Confederacy. His choosing it over the Union is one of the most famous American decisions. Maybe the only one that is more famous also involves slavery and rebellion: Huck Finn's decision to involve himself, *against* the dictates of his conscience ("All right, then, I'll *go* to hell"), in the flight of his friend Jim, a runaway slave, to freedom. This moment is Mark Twain's highest achievement, the central joke—Huck agonizes in his belief that he is doing bad as the reader is cheering him for doing good—in arguably the greatest American novel. Huck's good nature and his fellow feeling for Jim win out over all he has been taught (in particular by the moralizing Widow Douglas, Jim's owner) as a boy in the slave state of Missouri. Huck's choice is the opposite of Lee's. Huck's roots, of course, are not as deep as Lee's, and he, unlike Lee, is classless. But there is another great difference between the two.

In *Mark Twain: The Fate of Humor,* James M. Cox points out that Huck is not exchanging a false Old South conscience for a true Northern one. He is escaping from conscience altogether. For one thing, Huck and Jim mistakenly drift past the point at Cairo, Illinois, where Jim could have escaped onto free soil. Their raft takes them deeper into slave territory, and many critics have felt that the book goes downhill as it goes South. Cox argues that this is not a flaw in the book but its great "rebellion." Huck and the author are defying conscience, "which Mark Twain was later to rail at under the name of the 'Moral Sense.'" Throughout the book, "the conscience, whether it comes from society or from some apparent inner realm, is an agent of aggression—aggression against the self or against another." Huck "remains the fugitive—in flight from the old conscience and evading the development of a new one. And the reason he evades it is clear—the conscience is *uncomfortable*. Indeed, comfort and satisfaction are the value terms in *Huckleberry Finn*. Freedom for Huck is not realized in terms of political liberty but in terms of pleasure: 'You feel mighty free and easy and comfortable on a raft.'"

Lee consigned enjoyment of "comfort and ease" to colored folk. He "was never comfortable," his aide Walter Taylor complained, "unless he was uncomfortable." When he was in the field, adoring Virginia families often threw their homes open to him, but in those rare instances when he consented to spend the night under a roof, he always exasperated Taylor by his insistence on staying in the house's least comfortable room. Even his beloved Traveller had a choppy gait, which other men who tried to ride him, including Robert junior, found distinctly disagreeable. Outwardly Lee was cheerful, but what comforted him inwardly was his faith that his suffering was part of God's plan. "The most sublime word is duty"—what is owed—he said, a bankrupt's son. His duty was almost always grim. The word *lee* may mean "meadow" or "protected side," but Lee's conscience was a constant aggression against his own pleasure, against his own self.

In March 1870 Lee seemed older than his sixty-three years. He had always seemed more mature (and yet, more naive) than his age, but now his great visage was crumpled and the spring was gone from his step. He was presumably suffering from what is now called arteriosclerosis. Doctors prescribed warm weather and rest. And he wanted to visit his daughter Annie's grave before he died. So with her sister Agnes (Mildred stayed with her chickens; daughter Mary was off somewhere, no longer much connected to the family circle), he traveled by train to Savannah, stopping off in Richmond to brighten that grave with white hyacinths. Crowds and brass bands and mayors and town councils gathered to salute him at every stop. "Namesakes appeared," wrote Agnes, "of all sizes. Old ladies stretched their heads into the windows at way stations, and then drew back and said, 'He is mightily like his pictures.' . . . Wounded soldiers, servants, and working-men even. The sweetest little children—namesakes—dressed to their eyes, with bouquets of japonica—or tiny cards in their little fat hands—with their names." Was this what heaven would be like for a hero? Agnes found it delightful. Lee hated it. But then what does a Robert E. Lee get to do, at last, when he goes on to Glory? Lead cavalry charges?

Lee returned to Lexington weary and hurting, regretting the journey. Doctors prescribed lemon juice. On September 28 he presided over a three-hour church meeting. He came home, sat down to supper, and tried to say the blessing, but it

ROY BLOUNT, JR.

would not come. He had suffered what was probably a stroke. He couldn't speak coherently. He was helped into bed, where he lay mostly silent for nearly two weeks. Legend has it that he said, "Tell Hill he *must* come up," and, finally, "Strike the tent." Current medical analysis holds any such remarks to have been unlikely, but his doctors did record his saying, "It's no use" and then, later (perhaps he sensed others' concern and felt obliged to put a bright face on things), "I . . . feel . . . better." He died on the morning of October 12, 1870.

Almost immediately the Southern Historical Society, presided over by the cantankerous Gen. Jubal Early, whom Lee had called "my bad old man," and who—recently returned from flight to Mexico and then Canada—had mounted a campaign to enshrine Lee as an unconquerable combination of Siegfried and Christ. "We lost nearly everything but honor," Early had written to Lee, "and that should be religiously guarded." In a long, florid address on the second anniversary of Lee's death, Early declared, "It is a vain work for us to seek anywhere for a parallel to the great character which has won our admiration and love. Our beloved Chief stands, like some lofty column which rears its head among the highest, in grandeur, simple, pure and sublime." Those little feet that had been so lively were fixed to a pedestal.

Washington College became Washington and Lee University. Lifelong bachelor Custis was named president, but he served mostly as window dressing. "Have all the fun you can have," he advised one student. "I never had any fun in my life." He was closely attended by his valet, whom he called "my chamber maid, who is a man." The war he had spent in

Richmond, as an aide to Jefferson Davis, serving his father by keeping an eye on Mrs. Lee and on politics within the War Department. He had chafed in this role, yet twice declined offers to command troops in the field, doubting his own capacity though his father had advised him to try it and see—"until you come in the field you never will gain experience." In the last weeks of the war Custis had finally led a ragtag bunch of reservists and naval personnel into action, and those who didn't straggle acquitted themselves fairly well, considering, but they were all, Custis included, captured. Not long before, Robert, having grown corpulent, had written home to request new jackets: "Get any pattern to fit a big old man and cut them large. Measure Custis and give an extra size or two."

Robert's other sons, who had soldiered well, became fair-to-middling Lees of Virginia. (Rooney was elected to Congress, which probably would not have impressed his father.) There have been no more great ones.

Robert's wife lived on for a few years, her thoughts "ever in the past at Arlington—always Arlington." But if you got it back, a friend asked, what would you do with the Union graves? "My dear," she replied, "I would smooth them off and plant my flowers."

None of his daughters ever married.

APPENDIX I

Speculation

HE ELUDES US! He is vivid, and yet . . . he isn't there. Can it be because his austerity chastens us too much? Perhaps we can scratch his marble surface, jangle his composure, catch his flank in the air, if we indulge ourselves, just marginally, in fuzzy thinking and loose association.

A person is more than a union of two sets of genes. But how can we know Robert, when we know so much about his absent parent and so little about his real one? None of Ann Carter Lee's letters to Robert has been found, and the two to his brother Smith that do survive are not tender. "My dear Smith I have told you everything I thought interesting to you and now have arrived at the disagreeable point in my letter, the obligation I feel to chide you for never writing to your Mother more especially as her health is so impaired that you cannot calculate on ever seeing her again, but exclusive of my desire to hear from you I lament your dislike of writing because it will be such a disadvantage to you through life. . . . Oh that I could impart to you the knowledge gained from the experience of 54 years, then would you be convinced of the vanity of every pursuit not under the control of the most inflexible virtue." And so on.

She was an emotional, evangelical Episcopalian, which is hard to parse today. "Oh! Pray fervently for faith in Jesus Christ," she wrote to Carter when he was spending too much at Harvard. "He is the only rock of your salvation, and the only security for your resurrection from the grave!" She taught Robert his catechism before he could read. What was she like to cuddle with? Aside from the dream of inexhaustible fried chicken that Robert confided jocularly to Mary Chesnut and friends, only once do we get anything approaching a glimpse of him as voluptuary—in a recollection by Robert E. Lee Jr. of what Robert Sr. was like in and out of bed:

> He was always bright and gay with us little folk, romping, playing, and joking with us. With the older children, he was just as companionable, and I have seen him join my elder brothers and their friends when they would try their powers at a high jump. . . . The two younger children he petted a good deal, and our greatest treat was to get into his bed in the morning and lie close to him, listening while he talked to us in his bright, entertaining way. This custom we kept up until I was ten years old and over. . . . He was very fond of having his hands tickled, and, what was still more curious, it pleased and delighted him to take off his slippers and place his feet in our laps in order to have them tickled. Often, as little things, after romping all day . . . our drowsiness would soon show itself. . . . Then, to arouse us, he had a way of stirring us up with his foot—laughing heartily at and with us. . . . Sometimes, however, our interest in his wonderful

tales became so engrossing that we would forget to do our duty—when he would declare, "No tickling, no story!" When we were a little older, our elder sister told us one winter the ever-delightful "Lady of the Lake." Of course, she told it in prose and arranged it to suit our mental capacity. Our father was generally in his corner by the fire, most probably with a foot in either the lap of myself or youngest sister—the tickling going on briskly—and would come in at different points of the tale and repeat line after line of the poem—much to our disapproval—but to his great enjoyment.

The Carters, Ann's kin, were pleasure-loving people. If Ann had had no sensuous streak, she would never have fallen for Harry. If she, in her letters, stressed piety and inflexibility, perhaps it was because she was so keenly disposed to certain pleasures of the flesh. Jesus and his disciples washed one another's feet. Ann was often bedridden. Robert was presumably pleased to ease his mother's aches by massage.

Where did he get his lifelong leaning toward discomfort? Anachronistic as it may be, let us consider a widely popular late-twentieth-century book of psychology, Alice Miller's *The Drama of the Gifted Child*. Lee might have been a case study. Some of the most extraordinarily accomplished people, Miller argues, have managed to survive childhood abuse by means of the "gift" of a "numbness" that makes them capable of adapting to extreme pain.

There is no evidence that Lee suffered physical abuse (indeed, he probably suffered less of it than the average nineteenth-century child), but he did suffer insecurity, deprivation, and the burden of his father's shame, which carried with it the vivid image of a man beaten and slashed almost beyond recognition. And the parent he did have might well fit Miller's description of "a mother who at the core was emotionally insecure and who depended for her equilibrium on her child's behaving in a particular way." Such a mother was "dependent on a specific echo from the child that was essential to her, for she herself was a child in search of a person who could be available to her."

Lee himself fit the description of children who repress the childhood pain of having to serve as "mothers (confidantes, comforters, advisers, supporters) of their own mothers":

> They do well, even excellently, in everything they undertake; they are admired and envied . . . but behind all this lurks depression, a feeling of emptiness and self-alienation. . . . These dark feelings will come to the fore as soon as the drug of grandiosity fails . . . or whenever they suddenly get the feeling they have failed to live up to some ideal image or have not measured up to some standard. They are plagued by anxiety or deep feelings of guilt and shame.

It seems plausible that young Robert would have seen himself not as himself but as his mother's projection—the honorable, dependable, gallant lover she'd thought she was getting in Harry. A child can't be a *real* parent or spouse to his or her parent. He can only put on a parental or husbandly face. He may "develop in such a way that he reveals only what is expected of him and fuses so completely with what he reveals that one could scarcely guess how much more there is to him behind this false self. He cannot develop and differentiate his true self, because he is unable to live it."

The "gifted child," Alice Miller writes, develops extraordinary "antennae." He "has an amazing ability to perceive and respond intuitively, that is, unconsciously, to this need of the mother, or of both parents, for him to take on the role that had unconsciously been assigned to him." Perhaps such a child as an adult expects other people to have the same antennae, to instinctively act out their roles in the drama inbred in him. Especially if God is seen as the dramatist. Hence Lee's peculiar style of command, which failed at Gettysburg. His authority over his younger-generation lieutenants was based on their fond admiration of him and his faith in their imaginative response to his allusive, rather than direct and explicit, orders. Along with the loose reins came an unspoken threat of repudiation (when Lee decided that an officer in his command was a bad egg, he would arrange to have him transferred), but he was markedly disinclined to put his small foot down.

Many adults shaped by "gifted" childhoods, according to Miller, grew up in "families who were socially isolated and felt themselves to be too little respected in their neighborhood. They therefore made special efforts to increase their prestige with their neighbors through conformity and outstanding achievements. The child . . . was supposed to guarantee the family honor, and was loved only in proportion to the degree to which he was able to fulfill the demands of this family ideal by means of his special abilities, talents, his beauty, etc. If he failed he was punished . . . by the knowledge that he had brought great shame on his people."

This not to say that such people find no pleasure in life. As children "they [can] enjoy their encounters with nature, for example, without hurting the mother . . . reducing her power, or endangering her equilibrium." Lee always loved the outdoors, and animals, and foot massage.

When Custis was a boy, Lee took him for a walk in the snow. Custis trailed behind, placing his feet in his father's footprints. "When I saw this," Lee wrote a friend, "I said to myself, 'It behooves me to walk very straight, when this fellow is already following in my tracks.'" But Robert's feet were never more than a boy's. His shoe size, in full adulthood (and shoe sizes then were the same as now), was 4½ C. According to a Web site offering clothing advice for short men, the smallest men's athletic shoe that Nike, Reebok, Adidas, and several other shoe companies make today is 6½, and that has to be specially ordered. I don't know how big Ulysses Grant's feet were, or Napoleon's, say, but by way of more recent comparison we might consider Hack Wilson, who played baseball for the Chicago Cubs in the 1930s. He wore a size 5½ shoe, but he stood five foot six and had the upper body of a heavyweight (eighteen-inch neck) set on a jockey's legs. William Faulkner wore a 6½ (B or C), but he was five foot five and delicate overall. Nineteenth-century men were, of course, smaller generally than men today—average height during the Civil War was probably about five foot six—but Robert E. Lee was quite tall for the time, a strapping five foot ten and a half or five eleven. True, his height was disproportionately in his trunk (which made him, like his father, especially imposing on horseback), but nowhere near as much as

Hack Wilson's. No wonder in Lee's springy youth it appeared that his feet "spurned the ground upon which he trod."

And no wonder, as he aged, they craved attention. "Good bye, my precious child. My feet are entirely neglected," he writes his daughter Annie early in the war. Why, if they were *so* small, is their size neglected in all but the sculptor's reminiscences of him? Wouldn't such a large man be just a bit unsettled at having dainty feet?

We have no evidence that Lee and his wife, Mary, ever massaged each other's feet, but historians have often remarked on how obsessively their letters back and forth during the war dwell on the socks that Mary and friends knitted voluminously for him and his troops. Emory Thomas observes that

> within a sample of fourteen extant letters that he wrote his wife between January 10 and May 2, 1864, only one letter did not contain some reference to socks. Moreover, Lee pointed out that "There were 67 pairs . . . instead of 64, as you supposed"; "the number of pairs scarcely ever agrees with your statement"; "there were only 23 pairs & not 25 as you stated. I opened the bag and counted them myself twice."

No one has ascribed any psychosexual significance to this socks fixation (those who fault Lee for doing too little to keep his army supplied might point to it as an example of pennywise, pound-foolish micromanagement), but it must be said that in Lee's culture feet were highly eroticized. Mary Chesnut speaks often of Southern gentlemen's losing their heads over ladies' feet, concealed as they usually were by crinolines. The long adoring courtship of the great virginal beauty Sally "Buck" Preston by Gen. John Bell Hood ended when (while recuperating from the loss of one of his legs in battle) he was so overcome by the sight of her stockinged feet and ankles warming at the fire that he forgot himself and smooched her neck. Her honor impugned, she dropped him. Chesnut says of a young officer, "Today he was taking me to see Minnie Hayne's foot. He said it was the smallest, the most perfect thing in America! Now, I will go anywhere to see anything which can move the cool Captain to the smallest ripple of enthusiasm. He says Julia Rutledge knew his weakness and would not show him her foot. His Uncle James had told him of its arched instep and symmetrical beauty. So he followed her trail like a wild Indian, and when she stepped in the mud, he took a paper pattern of her track, or a plaster cast; something that amazed Miss Rutledge at his sagacity."

Of Lee's sexuality we can know only somewhat more than enough to find it as intriguing and off-putting as the belles of wartime Richmond did. But we can see that it was less gender-specific than that of his role model, George Washington, and we can gain some perspective on it by seeing how intriguing and off-putting were the belles, and incidentally the whores, of wartime Richmond. He was far more at ease among women (of his class), or with a child or two on a solemnly playful level, than among men. Yet many men seem to have had a kind of platonic crush on him.

As to Lee's crushes on young women, there was never any talk that Robert acted upon any of them. Compare the romantic life of Robert's ideal, George Washington. As a soldier of sixteen, he fell for eighteen-year-old Sally Fairfax, the recent bride of a friend of his. He wrote clumsily flirtatious letters to her. Only after he went into battle and emerged a hero did she write back—a confusing, tantalizing note signed by herself and two other ladies. He answered delightedly. With her friends, she paid him a visit. That was not what he had in mind. When he contracted a fever, she came alone to nurse him. He loved her company but decided she was teasing him. He became betrothed to Martha Custis, no stunner but always described as attractive and sweet. Sally, learning of his engagement, wrote him more letters that *seemed* flirtatious. His reply implied clearly enough that he would love to believe that she cared for him, but wondered whether "we still understand the true meaning of each other's letters." Her reply was oblique, and he wrote to her that he would not write to her again.

And he didn't until many happily married years later, when he and Martha both sent her friendly letters. By that time a Mrs. Bland, who had been out riding with George, had written to another lady, "General Washington throws off the hero and takes on the chatty, agreeable companion. He can be downright impudent sometimes. . . . Such impudence, Fanny, as you and I like." However, Martha had been along on the ride: "His worthy lady seems to be in perfect felicity when she is by the side of her *Old Man,* as she calls him." (Martha was one year older than George.)

When Washington was commanding the Revolutionary army, the Marquis de Lafayette wrote to him, "I have a wife, my dear general, who is in love with you. . . . She begs you would receive her compliments, and make them acceptable to Mrs. Washington." George replied, "Tell her . . . that I have a heart susceptible of the tenderest passion, and that it is already so strongly impressed with the most favorable ideas of her, that she must be cautious of putting love's torch to it, as you must be in fanning the flame. But . . . methinks I hear you say, 'I am not apprehensive of danger. My wife is young, you are growing old, and the Atlantic is between you.'"

When he was president, Washington received from a handsome widow an ode in his praise, and a coy request that he excuse her presumption. His reply asked for more poetry: "You see, Madam, when once the Woman has tempted us and we have tasted the forbidden fruit, there is no such thing as checking our appetites, whatever the consequences may be." But he was not "conscious of deserving anything more at your hands than the most disinterested friendship has a right to claim" and thanked her for sending her kind regards not only to him but to "the partner of all my domestic enjoyments."

Washington could compliment a lady, but always in a marital context, once he was married. When he was only engaged, he was willing to risk destroying his career and two stable marriages—his friends the Fairfaxes' and his own prospective one with Martha—by calling the hand of the woman to whom he was most strongly attracted. Washington when aroused was earnest, awkward, manipulable, dangerous. Lee when charmed was playful, graceful, extravagant, safe.

Lee's wife may soon have felt as uncherished as his mother had when newly married. Mary may well have been tempted to conclude that Robert had married her for her symbolic value. She was stuck with being an antebellum woman with no taste or perhaps aptitude for playing the belle, with no pleasure in housekeeping, with no way of being taken seriously as an artist or as anything else but a wife, with one baby after another finally amounting to seven, with real physical miseries, and with a husband who was usually apart from her and made *her* feel guilty about it—a husband who kept adjuring her in letters that while being sick was understandable, matter of course, really, she *must* be more diligent, stalwart, and fervently grateful to God for her blessings. That she must, in other words, be like his mother.

Perhaps he was not in the market for full-blown marital happiness. To a man who cherished independence and had been saddled as a child with too much responsibility for the emotional support of a woman with whom he could not find sexual release, connubial bliss might seem a delusion and a trap. (And let us not forget what happened to Harry—"one of the crucial compulsions of his character was mobility," writes Charles Royster—when he was trapped.) To the son of an absent father who was tainted by womanizing and from whom he had inherited both hot blood and shame, the role of a steady wife-lover might seem ungraspable, whereas the role of an unhappy but corporeally faithful husband might be a license to dally, detachedly, guiltlessly, with respectable ladies. His mother was a lone, lorn invalid; he married a woman who became one. He tried constantly to jolly them both, but perhaps with something of the same fatalism. In the current sense, he was an enabler to them, and they to him. Dutifulness and ardor are a hard combination for anyone to sustain.

For a man with Robert E. Lee's oedipal baggage, it may never even have *seemed* practicable.

The kisses Lee so freely sought from young ladies of his acquaintance and they so freely offered were, we may assume, on the cheek. Mary Chesnut writes of how appalled a friend ("a beautiful Jewess friend, Rachel we will call her whether it be her name or not") of a friend of hers was when, on a mission of mercy in a Richmond hospital, she was giving a sip of water to a wounded and apparently greatly weakened man, whom she assumed to be a gentleman, he was so handsome, quiet and clean—until he reached up and gave her a kiss on the lips. "Well she ought not to have put those red lips of hers so near &c&c&c," Chesnut quotes herself as telling the friend who carried the tale. The wounded man was a stranger, of course, but a kind of "Oh, my dear!" frisson runs through that diary entry, especially when we recall that "Buck" Preston, she of the beautiful little feet, took such dramatic offense when a man who was virtually her fiancé kissed her on the neck.

The wife of Gen. George Pickett told someone that "Lee was a great soldier and a good man, but I never wanted to put my arms around his neck, as I used to want to do to Joe Johnston." But if she was attracted to Pickett (long blond ringlets), Lee would not have been her type. *For the Love of Robert E. Lee,* a delightful 1992 novel by M. A. Harper, believably imagines Lee's being dragooned into adultery by an absent officer's wife at Fort Monroe in 1832, while cranky, unloved Mary is away at Arlington. The brief liaison fills him with guilt. In this novel the real love of his life, never consummated, is Markie Williams, the young woman to whom he

did write so feelingly, who did in fact avoid marriage until after Lee's death, and who, in the novel, keeps wishing he
would act upon their mutual urges. But that would have
meant scandal, divorce. Mightn't he rather have had a so-
phisticated wartime dalliance with Mary Chesnut's lovely
friend Constance Cary? Chesnut tells us of a party at the Jefferson Davises' around the autumn of 1863, when "we could
see General Lee holding the beautiful Miss Cary's hands in
the passage outside, though we could not hear what she was
saying." And then early in 1864 there is this:

> General Lee told us what a good son Custis was. Last night
> their house was so crowded Custis gave up his own bed to
> General Lee and slept upon the floor. Otherwise General
> Lee would have had to sleep in Mrs. Lee's room. She is a
> martyr to the rheumatism and rolls about in a chair. She
> can't walk.
>
> Constance Cary says, if it would please God to take poor
> Cousin Mary Lee—she suffers so—wouldn't these Richmond
> women *campaign* for Cousin Robert? In the meantime
> Cousin Robert holds all admiring females at arm's length.

Was Cousin Robert never tempted? In 1857, when he was stationed in Texas without his family, he wrote to his wife:

> There is a kind of widow here that I was going to recom-
> mend to Rooney. She seems to be a strong minded Ameri-
> can woman with the benefit of Texas habits. I was invited to
> her house to a musical party, but declined. About a week af-
> terwards, I thought it incumbent on me to return the com-
> pliment by a call. I found the house & made myself as

agreable as I could for about 5 minutes, when as I rose to depart, she took me out in her garden to see her corn & potatoes by *Starlight*. But she had waked up the wrong passenger.
I told her I had no knowledge of horticulture, & took no interest in agriculture in Texas. I have not seen her since, but I
think she has had some other musical parties. She has some
sons and daughters. She would take care of a man finely.
Those are the kind of women tell *Chass* a man wants in the
army.

A woman hardier than Mary . . . but surely Robert was not so
unkind as to be making that point, consciously. A woman for
Rooney. Who had just become engaged to his pretty young
cousin Charlotte Wickham, aka Chass. Lee worried, with reason, that Chass was too delicate to make a soldier's wife, and
he never seems to have been sure that his middle son had
sense enough to make large decisions. But twenty-year-old
Rooney didn't need this foxy-maternal widow, with her sons
and daughters and "Texas habits." Fifty-year-old Robert did.
The only way he knew to express his need was to inform poor
cranky Mary, no doubt to some extent jocularly, of his arch
indifference to the widow's "corn & potatoes by *Starlight*."
Soon he would take Chass to his foxy-paternal bosom.

One reason Lee fascinated smart-set Richmond women is
that his coolness was a match for theirs. The Chesnut diary
gives the impression that they found all men—not without
reason—faintly ridiculous. Another famous male flirt in that
circle was burly, gimpy Gen. Edward Johnson, a decade
younger than Lee but much less the Apollo. "He seemed per-
sistently winking one eye at you," wrote Chesnut, "but he

meant nothing by it. In point of fact he did not know it him-self." A tic from a war wound. "His head," wrote Chesnut, "is so strangely shaped—like a cone, an old fashioned beehive, or as Buck said: 'There is three tiers of it. It is like the pope's tiara.'" When he wasn't at war Johnson would go from one Richmond social occasion to another, proposing in a thun-derous voice to innumerable belles, who fended him off with taffy. Nine years after the war he died single.

Prostitutes were highly visible in the streets of Washing-ton during the Civil War. The Federal government trans-ported seventy of them to Richmond, along with other women of secessionist sympathies. Three months later the Confederate exchange agent returned two of the more obvi-ous professionals with a note to the appropriate Union offi-cial: "Sir: I send back to you two strumpets." Those who remained knew coarser generals than General Lee—for in-stance these clients mentioned by Clara A. of Richmond, in a diary brought to light by Thomas P. Lowry in *The Story the Soldiers Wouldn't Tell:*

General Limpy, the food fop—he must do the undressing. Shoes, too.

Four big generals last night came together. Red beard really has red hair all over. They brought two more barrels of wine and twenty blankets. Must sell some of the blankets. Have too many.

Redbeard brought the hero. I wondered why he came here, when he could get all he wanted free. All he can do is play.

Christ! The praying general was brought in today by Preacher H. He is rough and brutal. After I serviced him, he dropped to his knees and asked God to forgive me for my sins!

Lowry makes a circumstantial case that certain entries in this diary implicate John B. Hood, so he may have been wrong for Buck Preston. But the last we hear of Buck in Chesnut's diary, she is still rejecting suitors serially ("le roi est mort, vive le roi," as Chesnut puts it), and looking drawn. As for Chesnut, she wishes her husband weren't such a distant type, and often compares her marital state to slavery.

Jeb Stuart found time to cut a figure, "gayest of the gay," on the Richmond party scene, and he and his wife managed to conceive a child during the war, but he wrote to her that though he dreamed of "abandon" with her in a cozy post-war home—"I would step quietly into such a home and xxxxxxxxxxx"—their meetings during the war would have to be "unsatisfactory," their partings "abrupt." Custis Lee, who spent the war in Richmond as an officer on Jefferson Davis's staff, was a single man about town, but in the Chesnut diaries he mostly drops in here and there for a chat. Upon hearing that Custis had found nothing in her kitchen to sit on but a gridiron, Mrs. Davis asks, "Was he tender on the gridiron? He has never been known to be so anywhere else." Evidently wartime Virginia was not a great place for lovers, at least of the upper class.

Elvis and his mother made a great deal over each other's feet, calling them "sooties." Did Robert and his mother? We don't know. We do know that Lee incurred his only Civil War injury when, standing dismounted in the rain, he sprang to catch the bridle of his startled horse, Traveller, and tripped over some rubber overalls he was wearing (perhaps, when he was dismounted, they swaddled his feet?) and landed hard on his hands, breaking several small bones in the right one and badly spraining both wrists. For weeks both hands were in splints and the right one was in a sling, so that he had to be dressed and fed by "the graceful ministrations" (he wrote with tongue in cheek) of his servant Perry. For an hour, while a surgeon was being summoned to treat Lee in the field, a young member of Stonewall Jackson's staff, Henry Kyd Douglas, poured water over Lee's hands to ease the pain. Douglas noticed "what beautiful hands and feet he had and what a perfect figure: all parts of the handsomest man I ever saw."

If Douglas was nursing the hands (which we are told were very large), why was he struck equally by the (presumably shod) feet? Lee had a shy person's sensitivity to others' perceptions of him. How does it shape a young heterosexual man to know that his body parts have such aesthetic appeal for other men? This was a time, to be sure, when homoeroticism was regarded as such an unspeakable abomination that a respectable man could indulge in it without being suspected of it. But still. "By far the most magnificent man I ever saw," was the first impression of Charles Minor Blackford, a young officer in his army, and a month later, "he is the handsomest person I ever saw," and a year later, "the grandest looking man I ever saw," a man whom his troops regard with a "personal devotion 'passing the love of woman.'" Seventy years later his idolatrous biographer Douglas Southall Freeman would write (on what intimate authority it is hard to say): "In physique he was sound, without a blemish on his body."

Ulysses S. Grant in his youth was such a rosy-cheeked sylph that his nickname at West Point was "Beauty." In maturity, according to a fellow officer, Grant had "a girlish modesty." His future sister-in-law called him "pretty as a doll." Grant developed a severe slouch, made a point of dressing sloppily, grew a coarse dark beard, and took up the whiskey that nearly destroyed his career and the cigars that eventually killed him. (Cast as Desdemona in a sportive army production of *Othello* while stationed in Texas with Zachary Taylor's army in 1845, he failed to convince—was he really trying?—and had to be replaced by a professional actress.)

Lee, blessed with a manlier beauty, did nothing to efface it, certainly, and was wistful to see it fade. When his daughter-in-law Charlotte wrote to ask how he was holding up during the war, he responded, "I have the same handsome hat which surmounts my gray head . . . and shields my ugly face, which is masked by a white beard . . . stiff and wiry. . . . In fact, an uglier person you have never seen, and so unattractive is it to our enemies that they shoot at it whenever visible to them, but though age with its snow has whitened my head, and its frosts have stiffened my limbs, my heart, as you well know, is not frozen to you." As he aged, his hair retreated, and he began parting it in the back and bringing it forward, as did Ernest Hemingway late in life.

Lee's mother, from whom he inherited his beauty, can't have felt that her looks brought her happiness. Very beautiful women, whose authority derives from skin-deep attributes, are often deeply doubtful of their self-worth. So was Lee. Whereas your standard Virginia cavalier buck took "honour" as a pretext for dueling, lording it over inferiors, and raising

Cain, Lee took it as a commitment to purity, to something finer than himself–the self against which his mother's preachments and his father's bad example constrained him to protect his virtue.

Gifted children, writes Alice Miller, are "never really free," because they are dependent on admiration, which can never satisfy them because what everyone really needs is to be loved for his or her own imperfect, angry, jealous, anxious self. They are restless perfectionists, always ready to feel guilt and shame. They have learned to seem calm and cheerful, but inside they swing back and forth between grandiosity–not *feeling* grand, because they are driven to present themselves in the ideal light by which they judge themselves harshly–and depression: "the defense against the deep pain over the loss of self that results from denial."

So nowadays self-denial is pathological. At some point in the future this assumption may seem as dated as Lee's unreflective belief in self-denial seems today. Life will never fit into the parameters of psychotherapy until everyone has it and it works. But Lee would seem to fit Miller's profile.

He could be forthrightly aggressive against others, but only when they were faceless–"those people" who were trying to take over his state. Miller writes that "gifted" children in adulthood, "in an unconscious thrust for revenge, may engage in acts of violence. . . . Such acts are often done in the name of 'patriotism' or religious beliefs.'" Or they "actively continue the torture once inflicted upon them in selfscourging." Lee was not a natural antagonist, because he generally "acted in"–as psychologists today say disturbed girls tend to do, whereas disturbed boys "act out." That is to say, disturbed boys are more likely to wreak violence on others, whereas disturbed girls turn anger and fear in on themselves in the form of depression or self-mortification.

What if Harry had come back from the debacle in Baltimore and said to his little boy, "You should see the other fellows. I'll get over this, son, and we'll go fishing"? Robert might not have associated manliness with suffering and loss. He might, like Stuart and Jackson, have been able to take simpleminded pleasure in heartily aggressive Christian honor.

Can self-denial be a tragic flaw? If Lee is a tragic hero, you would think someone would have come close, at least, to portraying him as such in fiction. In Thomas Keneally's *Confederates,* Jackson comes alive, but Lee sounds tinny, has no texture. In *The Killer Angels,* Michael Shaara's rattling good, factually coherent novel about Gettysburg, Lee rings hollow. In *Patriotic Gore* Edmund Wilson compares Grant and Lee, respectively, to Ahab and that great void, the white whale.

Someday, maybe, Lee will come alive on the screen. Marlon Brando played Robert E. Lee Clayton in *Missouri Breaks,* wearing a voluminous housedress on horseback, and Montgomery Clift was Robert E. Lee Prewitt in *From Here to Eternity.* (Not all the many notable nonfictional Americans whose middle name is Lee—Jerry Lee Lewis, Kathie Lee Gifford, John Lee Hooker—can have been named for the Confederate hero, but Robert Lee Frost, the poet, was, and Lee Harvey Oswald's first name came from his father, Robert E. Lee Oswald.)

In the Ken Burns's Civil War documentary, the voice of the late Jason Robards Jr. seems just right as that of Ulysses S. Grant. Lee's voice is done by a man named George Black, with whose other work I am not familiar. Grant appears in old movies fairly vigorously at times. Yes, Harry Morgan's Grant in *How the West Was Won* is silly, but at least Grant gets a scene and dialogue (with John Wayne's equally silly William Tecumseh Sherman). Lee in the cinema has generally been no more than a blip of rigid dignity. Jim (or James) Welch, who portrayed him in two silent films, was a bit player. Howard Gaye, who pops up briefly as Lee in *Birth of a Nation*, and Hobart Bosworth, who does the same in the 1930 *Abraham Lincoln*, both played Christ in silents (Bosworth in something called *Business Is Business*, Gaye, uncredited, in *Intolerance*). In *Santa Fe Trail*, 1940, which despite its title culminates in the attack on John Brown, Jeb Stuart gets to be played by Errol Flynn, and George Custer (who wasn't even there in real life) by an extremely lean-jawed Ronald Reagan; Lee is played, peripherally, by a potato-faced fellow (if a potato can be bearded, which Lee wasn't at the time, and vaguely fussy-looking) named Moroni Olsen, who also played Pope Leo I in *Sign of the Pagan* and the voice of the senior angel (uncredited) in *It's a Wonderful Life*. Don't be misled by the movie-channel trailer for *They Died with Their Boots On*, which includes clips of "Grant!" fuming and "Lee!" on a rearing horse—the latter turns out to be Regis Toomey as Robert's nephew Fitzhugh.

To be sure, we have Martin Sheen in *Gettysburg*. It's a humanized version of Lee, derived from *The Killer Angels*, but in this case humanizing is condescending, as when Lee spoke of humanizing the Comanche Indians. At any rate Gettysburg is hardly Lee at his best. And Martin Sheen? He was fine as the young serial killer in *Badlands*, and he makes an engaging president of the United States on the TV series *West Wing.* But as Marse Robert? A Lee short in the saddle, who *discernibly* gets off on being regarded as a demigod? No. Most of the best Civil War historians may have been Southern, but the victors have apparently been the casting directors.

However, I write this before the release of the television film *Gods and Generals,* which promises what should be easily the best movie portrayal of Lee—by Robert Duvall. This is a rare case of the actor's being less beautiful than the historical character, but the prospect is still exciting. I want to envisage a Lee in whom Duvall brings together aspects of the hard-riding, stalwart, twinkle-in-the-eye Augustus McCrae in *Lonesome Dove;* the steely, recessive, un-Italian consigliere in *The Godfather;* the truly and personally religious, volatile, free-lancing preacher in *The Apostle;* the horsey, daughter-loving, exasperating father in *Something to Talk About;* the overbearing military father in *The Great Santini;* the kind, manly, female-friendly father in *Rambling Rose;* the spooky but decent Boo Radley in *To Kill a Mockingbird.* Trouble is, Duvall won't have much to work with when it comes to the coarse, selfish aspects that make these characters so tangy. The film is said to focus primarily on Stonewall Jackson, a character who *enjoyed* being himself.

Most American icons, whatever their self-destructive tendencies, have an abundance of what Lee seemed to make himself do without: the capacity to appreciate, celebrate, and advance themselves. Take two other mother's boys, Mark Twain and Elvis. Like Lee they were haunted by death and had dissociative relations with women, but their mothers indulged them more as boys (Sam Clemens as a naughty one,

Elvis as a chosen one), and as men they made no bones about fluffing their feathers. (Also, each of them in his way was boosted, crucially, by a great appreciation of African-American culture, which Lee utterly lacked.)

The most sympathetic nonhistorical depictions of Lee's character are by women. In *The Wave,* Evelyn Scott's under-recognized 1929 novel of the war, we get a couple of oblique but poignant glimpses. "Lee's kindly, rather chilling eyes rested, specifically, on nobody, yet he interrogated all, with that naively disguised eagerness which made all hesitate guiltily before replying, since they could not honestly concur in the utterance of even this temperately hopeful opinion." He is revered, but inside he is depressed, self-reproaching, self-flagellating, even. On the outside, equable: "that persistent calm which, for some reason, aroused in his inferiors an unwilled, and even disrespectful, pity." Tragedy is supposed to *purge* pity.

Emory Thomas writes that "the best portrait of Robert E. Lee in American fiction" is the aforementioned *For the Love of Robert E. Lee.* M. A. Harper gives us Lee as a sad but winning *romantic* hero, in the historically well-grounded imagination of the narrator, a spunky teenage Southern liberal girl who in 1963, a hundred years after Gettysburg, falls in love with his portrait—the one painted of him in 1851, when he was at his most beautiful. Harper is a Southern woman whose photograph suggests that she might have been that girl in the 1960s. Her novel locates Lee's lifelong dissatisfaction in an imagined deathbed confession by his mother—as he "smooths her wilted hair under the lace cap"—that she didn't want him when he was born.

APPENDIX II

Lee's Humor

EMORY THOMAS CONCLUDES that Lee was a tragic hero with a comic view of life. He cites the time, after the war, when Lee received a "superb afghan" and a tea cozy in the mail from a Scottish admirer. "Lee opened the parcel, draped the afghan about his shoulders, donned the tea cozy as a helmet, and commenced to dance to the tune Mildred was playing on the piano." When Lee confided this to a female friend, she told her sister how shocked she was that *"our hero"* would cavort so childishly and in such a getup.

Aside from the sternness of Lee's mother's surviving letters, the only trace of her personality that comes down to us from her time is the reference to her "grave humor." We might see that humor reflected in Alice Miller's observation that "a mother cannot respect her child as long as she does not realize what deep shame she causes him with an ironic remark, intended only to cover her own uncertainty." Lee's humor was friendlier than that, but the irony involved could be unsettling.

In his monumental biography Douglas Southall Freeman wrote, "Lee's correspondence does not contain the echo of a liaison, the shadow of an oath, or the stain of a single obscene suggestion." Freeman's blood must have run cold a year after *Lee* was published, when he obtained from an autograph dealer a letter he had not seen before. Lee had written it at the age of twenty-eight, in the summer of 1835 when he was surveying the Ohio-Michigan border. It was addressed to "Mon Ami"—a fellow engineering officer, Lt. George Washington Cullum. Amid joshing personal notes, Lee is suddenly moved to "confess an act of indiscretion." It seemed that he and a colleague, Lt. Washington Hood, had in the course of their surveying entered a locked lighthouse through the window,

> when we discovered the keeper at the door. We were warm & excited, he irascible & full of venom. An altercation ensued which resulted in his death. . . . We have nothing to offer in our behalf, but *necessity* and as we found the Lt. House in a most neglected condition and shockingly dirty . . . I hope it will not be considered that we have lopped from the Government a useful member, but on the contrary—to have done it some service, as the situation may now be more efficiently filled and we would advise the New Minister to make choice of a better Subject than a d——d [*sic*] Canadian *Snake*.

Surely here was not only the shadow of an oath, but a confession of at least complicity in murder. Freeman wrote nothing about the matter until ten years later, when a troubled historian at the Detroit Public Library who had seen a copy of the letter and assumed it to be spurious wrote to ask Freeman's opinion. The original was undoubtedly in Lee's handwriting, Freeman replied, and "internal evidence seems to suggest that the lighthouse keeper was killed by General Lee's companion. . . . General Lee . . . always acknowledged his own responsibilities, but when responsibilities were coupled with someone else, he took pains to use an indirect form of discourse that would not put the blame on the other man though the language was so shaped that he did not, himself, assume the blame."

In 1949, anticipating a new printing of *Lee,* Freeman felt honor bound to send the publisher this footnote: "An unhappy incident of Lee's experience on this survey was the accidental death of a Canadian lighthouse keeper 'in a scuffle' over the use of his tower. . . . A search of Canadian records yields no details."

Freeman went to his death under the burden of this interpretation. But in 1977 historian John L. Gignillat took a look at the letter, went out and studied the remains of the lighthouse, scoured local history, and came to what now seems the obvious conclusion: Lee had been kidding. The lighthouse keeper, the lopped member, was—literally—a snake.

Lee as a young man, a male friend wrote, could hold forth at length so merrily as to make his friends "laugh very heartily" while he himself laughed "until the tears ran down his face." An officer who served with him said "his white teeth and winning smile were irresistible," but neither teeth nor smile appear in portrait or photograph of him. His jocular side, however, is well documented. Once, during his first posting in Washington, as he rode through town on horseback he spied a friend and cried, "Climb aboard!" They proceeded down Pennsylvania Avenue, waving to friends. As they passed the White House they encountered Secretary of the Treasury Levi Woodbury, who (and this is what makes the joke) stood astonished as the two-on-a-horse bowed to him.

From his letters home just before and just after Cold Harbor, a literal-minded reader might conclude that Lee was troubled less by the miseries of impending defeat, or even by thoughts of his late daughter Annie, than by his daughter Mildred's having acquired a pet squirrel, which she named Custis Morgan, after her brother and the Confederate raider for whom "Morgan's mule" was named.

That squirrel is going to bite somebody badly, Lee keeps insisting, as though from experience, in at least six different letters. Better hold Custis's head underwater during his bath, Lee suggests—or convert him to "squirrel soup thickened with peanuts. Custis Morgan in such an exit from the stage would cover himself with glory." Set against the moaning dying thousands at Cold Harbor, not to mention the despoiling of Lee's native countryside, Lee's expression of relief, finally, that the demonized squirrel has escaped "into his native woods" is as chilling a small bit of American humor as has ever survived in print.

In Lee's letters to his wife he rarely indulged in levity, but with Markie Williams and other ladies he gossiped wittily, fancifully: "Mr. Daniels is wrapped up in his blushes and philosophy," and "Mr. Gibson's lady love has found one more to her liking . . . & he has consoled himself with a *horse*." To yet another of his pen pals, the lovely Tasy Beaumont, he wrote of a lovestruck mutual friend, "Comfort him Tasy, for if the fire of his heart is so stimulating to the growth of his whiskers there is danger of his being suffocated. . . . I hope the sympathy between himself and Miss Louise is not so intimate as to produce the same effect on her, for I should hate her sweet face to be hid by such hairs unless they were . . . mine."

One morning in the winter of 1862, Lee's staff could not help but notice the delivery of a demijohn to their commander's tent. Knowing well his openhandedness in the sharing of delicacies on the one hand, and his unreceptiveness to alcoholic beverages on the other (he probably took a sip of blackberry wine or brandy occasionally for his aches and pains, but more than once he urged Mary *not* to forward a gift of nice liquor some civilian supporter had given her to send to him), the staff speculated thirstily among themselves as to what fine spirit this jug might hold. At lunchtime Lee came out and said, "Perhaps you gentlemen would like a glass of something?" Their mouths watering, they went to the mess tent, where the demijohn was tipped and each man's cup was filled—with, they saw to their dismay, Lee's favorite drink, buttermilk. His near-teetotaler's amusement was greater than theirs. This was so in other instances of his arch, if effectively tolerant, jocularity regarding his inferiors' taste for strong drink. He clearly had no sympathy for the notion that taking a belt could be pleasurable. Nor did he see the appeal of barracks humor. Whereas Washington had a strong head for madeira and, judging from some of his letters, enjoyed bluff double-entendre.

So how about the "Pussyism" joke? When Lee's daughter Mildred, after the war, responded to a young woman friend's invitation with a note saying, "*Waffles—Pussy—*and *Mr. Harrison* are temptations too strong to resist," she was undoubtedly referring straightforwardly to a cat or to some friend with a nickname. But can the word *pussy* have connoted nothing sexual to her father the soldier? (We do know that one of his first steps as executor of his father's estate was to change the long-standing name of one of the plantations involved, Romancock, to Romancoke, for reasons of propriety.) According to J. E. Lighter, editor of the *Random House Historical Dictionary of American Slang,* although there is no written evidence of such a connotation before 1879, the chances are that it was current in the 1840s, at least in some circles—but probably not, Lighter believes, in Lee's. After talking to Lighter, I came upon *The Story the Soldiers Wouldn't Tell: Sex in the Civil War,* by Thomas P. Lowry, in which he quotes a "civil-war era" pornographic verse-novel that includes these lines: "one, more wanton than the rest / Seized on love's moss-bounded nest. / And cried, 'Poor puss shall have a treat / For the first time of juicy meat." But given Lee's character, it seems likely that his sense of the Pussyism pun was innocent enough that he might have shared it with his mother.

And yet there is surely something disproportionate about the Marble Model's delight in this particular play on words. Can he have been so pleased with a small venture into raciness that he couldn't get over it? Anti-Jacksonians often lack an easy way with off-color language. The occasional leakage of a *keister* reference by Ronald Reagan, or "We kicked a little ass" by the elder George Bush, may serve as late-twentieth-century examples. But Richard Nixon's compensatory flaunting of between-us-regular-guys dirty talk was well beneath Lee. We need not assume that he was being in any degree smutty, to find a gender issue in this joke.

According to Lighter, *pussy* in the sense of *sissy* is of mid-twentieth-century vintage. But Mark Twain includes in his *Library of Humor* a sketch by George William Curtis, first published in 1854, which satirizes a Puseyite: the Rev. Cream Cheese, who "not only has such aristocratic hands and feet, in the parlor, but . . . is so perfectly gentlemanly in the pulpit." He is able to "talk beautifully for about twenty minutes" when asked for advice on what color velvet a lady's prayer-book should be bound in, taking into account "the violet and scarlet capes of the cardinals, and purple chasubles, and the lace edge of the Pope's little short gown." He flirts with the narrator, a Mrs. Potiphar, in an unfleshly sort of way, after describing himself as "an unworthy candidate, an unprofitable husband." He warns against hiring "a footman with insufficient calves." Puseyism would seem to have been associated with effeminacy.

And for centuries *puss* and *pussy* have been applied to girls and women. The *Oxford English Dictionary* cites, from 1583, "You shall have every sawcy boy . . . to catch up a woman & marie her. . . . So he have his pretie pussie to huggle [hug] withall," and from *Uncle Tom's Cabin*, "'What do you think, pussy?' said her father to Eva." With the "Pussyism" sally and his twitting of jug lovers Lee was not trying to emulate rough male joking; on the contrary, he was mocking it, as a clever woman might, who can more than hold her own among men without descending to their level. We may assume that Lee (a Low Churchman himself—the Whig Party was founded in England in opposition to Catholicism) was more comfortable than the other officers with his feminine side, and enjoyed twitting their discomfort.

In England, according to John Shelton Reed in *Glorious Battle: The Cultural Politics of Victorian Anglo-Catholicism,* Puseyism was derided as "a female movement," and not just in objection to incense and lavish vestments. Puseyism was widely seen as a threat to Victorian family values—that is, to patriarchal authority. Revival of the confessional horrified insecure autocrats of the hearth, who couldn't bear the thought of their daughters and wives exposing intimate secrets to, and receiving God knew what kind of advice from, unmarried priests—in a *booth.* Robert E. Lee had grown up in the image of the idealized George Washington and in the bosom of an intense, independent woman. He knew that a man could get along without an earthly father. And why should women make him apprehensive? Women, his wife excepted, brought out his light side. It was men, beginning with his father, who let him down.

APPENDIX III

Lee's Attitude Toward Slavery

It is a simple matter to conclude that Lee, however high-minded, was an evildoer because he fought for slavery. Slavery was indeed evil, but let us not be glibly judgmental. Lee was born into the slavocracy, as a soldier he had only marginal involvement in it, and he can hardly be expected to have figured out a way to reengineer the economy or the population of the South. But let us compare him in this regard with Ulysses S. Grant.

Grant too was implicated in slavery. The father of his wife, Julia, was a downright belligerently proud slave-owning Missourian. At one point during the war, Julia writes in her memoirs, she visited her father and fretted as he

> argued and argued with me constantly upon the constitutionality of secession. I was dreadfully puzzled about the horrid old Constitution anyway, and once, when quite worn out with listening, said: "Papa, why don't they make a new Constitution since this is such an enigma—one to suit the times, you know. . . . We have steamers, railroads, telegraphs, etc." He looked at me aghast and left me, saying

with a groan, "Good Heavens! If Old Jackson had been in the White House . . . he would have hanged a score or two of [abolitionists], and the country would have been at peace."

All through the war Julia was attended by personal slaves she had brought with her from Missouri. The Emancipation Proclamation had freed the slaves in the Confederate states, but not until a law was passed after Lincoln's death, and ratification of the Thirteenth Amendment later in 1865 established that law's constitutionality, would slavery be illegal in the United States as a whole. In fact, when she left her residence in Maryland to visit Richmond after the fall of that city to Union forces just before the end of the war, she was accompanied by a servant, Eliza, who on entering Virginia became the only legal slave in the South. "I only saw that the city was deserted; not a single inhabitant visible," Mrs. Grant wrote in her memoirs. "Only now and then we would meet one or two carriages with visitors from the North, coming like ourselves to see this sad city, and occasionally an old colored servant would pass along, looking on us as intruders, as we all felt we were." Apparently Mrs. Grant did not regard servants as inhabitants, but neither did she consider her slaves to be bound. Her nurse, also named Julia, had left her service earlier rather than accompany her to visit the Missouri relatives, "as I suppose she feared losing her freedom."

Grant himself, however, openly disagreed with his father-in-law well before the war. And while it is impossible to picture Lee beating a slave (as far as we know he never lifted a hand in violence to anybody), we have accounts of Grant, as

a civilian before the war, refusing to whip his wife's slaves for
disobedience when she wanted him to, and intervening to
stop a neighbor from whipping a slave, and telling his wife's
slaves directly that he would free them as soon as he could,
and saying to a neighbor who suspected one of his in-laws'
slaves of disloyalty, "I don't know why a black skin may not
cover a true heart as well as a white one." There is no record
of Lee's having ever made such an evenhanded assessment of
the two races. As a young man Lee was attended by slaves, he
nursed one who was dying, he worried from a distance about
the welfare of others. As a young man trying to make a go of
farming in Ohio (after abandoning a blighted career in the
peacetime army), Grant found it necessary to rent two slaves
and to buy one, William Jones, from his father-in-law. He
worked closely with Jones in the fields. When he gave up
farming, he freed Jones with no compensation to himself, at
a time when his own financial situation was precarious and
Jones could have been sold for a considerable amount of
cash.

But then Grant had been brought up, in the hardscrabble
Midwest, by an attentive father who later claimed he had
moved out of Kentucky when slavery spread into that state,
because he couldn't stand being around the kind of people
who made slaves do their work for them. Jesse Grant, the father, wrote verse for an abolitionist publication, and Ulysses
was a good friend of the son of that publication's editor.

A more pertinent comparison is between Lee's attitude
toward slavery and that of his cavalier model, George Washington. Instead of assuming that slaves were not ready for
freedom, as Lee did, Washington concluded that slavery was

keeping them from developing their natural human propensity for honorable ambition. In the 1790s he spent two years trying to work out a system whereby his lands could be administered in such a way as to "liberate a certain species of property which I possess, very repugnantly to my own feelings." His will freed all of his slaves so ungradually (at the death of his wife) that his estate had to be broken up and even his house, Mount Vernon, had to be rescued and maintained by a historical association.

In colonial Virginia, there was a law against freeing even one's own slaves, in part to keep owners from dumping them when they got too old to work. But after the Revolution it was pretty much the accepted thing for a great man of Virginia to provide for the manumission, and financial support where necessary, of his slaves at his death—as long as they were sent out of the state. In 1833 John Randolph, the great Virginian orator, congressman, and scholar, did this orally on his deathbed. Since he was required by law to do so in the presence of a white witness who would then remain with him until his death, he ordered his old retainer John to lock the protesting family physician into the deathbed chamber. Liberty as a gift, largess to faithful servants.

As Kenneth S. Greenberg points out, "Because one of the distinguishing characteristics of a master was the ability to give gifts, and one of the distinguishing characteristics of a slave was the inability to give gifts, an emancipation that assumed the form of a gift paradoxically reconfirmed the master-slave relationship." It seems an easy sort of generosity for a man to enjoy the service of slaves all his life and then to impose on his heirs the trouble of ushering these valuable assets into freedom, but that must have been what was meant by "gradual emancipation," which Lee after the war maintained he had always been in favor of. (In her diary Mary Lee looked forward to a day when all the family slaves could be sent to Africa. She told her body servant Eliza that she could have her freedom, in due time, if she would go there. Lee expressed skepticism as to this project's practicality. In 1860 Mary wrote that Eliza was free and living in Newport, Rhode Island.)

One of Ann Carter Lee's forebears, Robert Carter, decided in his old age to record a deed of gradual emancipation under which his 500 or so slaves were to pass temporarily to his heirs, who were, however, required each year to free every slave who had reached adulthood during the year. His family was outraged by this arrangement, and some of the heirs refused to honor it. It's hard to see how gradual emancipation could ever have gathered much momentum, when for instance Virginia responded to the Nat Turner rebellion by making it illegal for slaves to preach or assemble, and stiffening penalties against teaching slaves to read. (Mary Lee and her daughters, however, did some sub-rosa schooling of Arlington's slave children—Agnes in her journal referred to them as "'ebony mites,' as Papa calls them.")

As a professional soldier, Lee had no business engaging in political controversy. But he was personally against slavery the way a Nike executive might personally be against Indonesian sweatshops if he had to feed, clothe, and house the workers and live surrounded by them—*Isn't there some way we can do without these people?* Like Lincoln, Lee was favorably disposed toward the relocation of freedmen to Africa, and he may in fact have transported to Liberia some slaves he had no use for. But exportation, fortunately for the future of American culture, was not a viable solution. So Lee did have recourse to one morally defensible, and practically quite considerable, point. "The best men of the South"—that is, prominent white conservatives—"have long desired to do away with the institution and were quite willing to see it abolished," Lee stated (not for publication) after the war. "But . . . the question has ever been: What will you do with the freed people?" It was not as though they could readily breathe the air of freedom in the North. There was plenty of discrimination up there. When a group of slaves freed by John Randolph's will tried to settle in Ohio, they were driven away by a mob. But there is something bloodless and cranky about Lee's disapproval of slavery—as if it were primarily a management problem.

Lee never referred to human chattel as "the slaves," nor "the darkies" (as a white man in the deeper South might have) but always as "the people." Often, to be sure, with a possessive, which referred not to themselves but to their owners. "I trust you will so gain the affection of your people," he wrote before the war to a slaveholding friend whose home had been damaged by a fire of perhaps suspicious origin, "that they will not wish to do you any harm." In other letters he refers to "her people," "his people." But never "my" or even "our" people. Light-Horse Harry had fought for the liberty of "we, the people." He was no populist, but for his son Robert "the people" very nearly meant "those people." Nearly but not quite. By referring to the slaves at Arlington as "the people at Arlington," he managed to distance himself, somewhat, from both proprietariness and renunciation. "Those people" was what he would call the people he fought against in the Civil War.

The slaves Lee had amiable contact with were house servants, in a context of gentility. A colonial memoirist tells a story of a slave owner who so enjoyed watching his people's singing and dancing at night that his wife pouted. "I think you think more of those slaves than you do of me." If she didn't like the entertainment, her husband told her, she should get on back to the house. It is impossible to picture Lee seeking such enjoyment (or Mary accepting such a rebuke). What about the prevalent practice of masters' visiting the quarters at night for perquisite sexual release? "God forgive us," Mary Chesnut exclaimed in her diary, "but ours is a monstrous system. . . . Any lady is ready to tell you who is the father of all the mulatto children in everybody's household but her own." But Lee was never in any such seigneurial situation, and he was not a brutal or lecherous man. When there were lady houseguests at Arlington after Mr. Custis's death, and Lee was staying there himself, he would go into the garden before breakfast, pick roses, and lay a fully bloomed one at each lady's plate, a bud at each girl's.

Thomas Jefferson, who is generally held to have sired children half slave and half free, worried that as Virginia planters' children mingled freely with slave children, the former would turn tyrannical. "The whole commerce between master and slave is a perpetual exercise of the most boisterous passions, the most unremitting despotism on the one part, and degrading submissions on the other. Our children see this, and . . . cannot but be stamped by it with odious peculiarities."

Lee, thanks to his father's profligacy, had grown up with no such sense of entitlement. In the matter of slave management as in so many other matters, he had a negative model to live down. In Light-Horse Harry's days of financial distress, a story went around about his asking a neighbor to lend him a horse. The neighbor did so, it was said, and also sent along a servant on a second horse, either for Harry's convenience or so the neighbor could be sure of getting the horse back. The servant didn't return for weeks, and when he did he was on foot and much the worse for wear. Harry had sold both horses, the servant said. But why had it taken the servant so long to get home? "'Cause General Lee sold me too."

Apocryphal white humor, perhaps, of an incidental Mr. Bones sort that Robert E. Lee never, so far as we know, indulged in. In his letters home during the war he often mentions that his black servants in the field, Meredith and Perry, are well and "send their respects to all." He does not find them comical. Once he grumbles that "Perry is very willing and I believe does as well as he can. You know he is slow & inefficient & moves much like his father Lawrence, whom he resembles very much. He is also very fond of his blankets in the morning. The time I most require him out. He is not very strong either." But although there is in that a suggestion of you-know-how-these-people-are, there is also a good deal, it seems to me, of genuine fondness and familiarity. Were we to let our twenty-first-century sympathies drift noblesse-obligeward we might—almost—make the case that slavery *was* harder on Robert E. Lee, subjectively, than on at least those slaves for whom he took responsibility. "The poor blacks have a multitude of miseries," he wrote once to his wife. "I hope the death that must come sooner or later will end them all." He seems to have felt that way often about himself.

We may wonder what became of the slaves that Mary Custis Lee's father left–along with the provision that they be emancipated within five years–to the Lees when he died (before the war). Did any of them, or their descendants, take the name of Lee? An apropos study in nomenclature is Samuel, a coffee-colored man who had only that name in slavery but was probably the unacknowledged son of Gen. Samuel McGowan, a distinguished brigade commander under Lee. Young Samuel, who attended McGowan in camp and on the battlefield, was himself wounded twice. During Reconstruction he became speaker of the South Carolina House of Representatives and a trustee of the University of South Carolina. His influence opened the university to black students, but that policy died when Reconstruction did, and he fell back on a hardscrabble law practice. He had taken the name, not of Samuel McGowan Jr., but of Samuel J. Lee.

In fact a glance at *American National Biography* would suggest that the most notable Lees (not to mention Washingtons) since the Civil War have been black. George E. and Julia Lee, brother and sister, were Kansas City jazz pioneers– George a prominent bandleader and Julia a singer of spicy songs like "I Didn't Like It the First Time (But Oh How It's Grown on Me)," which pretends to be about spinach but isn't, and "(Come and See Me Baby, But Please) Don't Come Too Soon." Then there's Ulysses Grant Lee Jr., born in Washington, D.C., in 1913. He went on to become an educator, coeditor with Sterling Brown of *The Negro Caravan* (for many years the standard anthology of African-American writing), and an army officer who wrote the definitive study of the distinction achieved by, and the discrimination practiced against, African-American troops during World War II.

BIBLIOGRAPHY

ONE STUDY OF LEE lists an even two hundred others as essential reading, and that list is out of date.

Douglas Southall Freeman's four-volume *R. E. Lee*, first published in 1934–35, is a monument to Lee and to Freeman's twenty years of research. But Freeman insists that "there is no inconsistency to be explained, no enigma to be solved" in Lee, whose character's "essential elements . . . were two and only two, simplicity and spirituality." In principle that is true of, say, water, but go find a river that pure.

The definitive biography is Emory M. Thomas's 1995 *Robert E. Lee*, which acknowledges the stature and precedence of Freeman's work but greatly corrects it in light of further research and due contemporary process. Thomas is considerably and considerately shorter-winded than Freeman, and a master of chapterization: the beginnings, endings, and titles of his chapters are inspired.

I also enjoyed and profited from a thorough perusal of Margaret Sanborn's *Robert E. Lee: A Portrait* (1966), which engagingly brings out the man's feminine side.

The principal revisionists of Freeman, coming before Thomas's balanced portrayal, are Thomas L. Connelly, whose 1977 study of the mythification of Lee, *The Marble Man: Robert E. Lee and His Image in American Society,* is first rate, and Allen T. Nolan, who makes an overly dismissive but not dismissible case against Lee's nobility in his *Lee Considered: General Robert E. Lee and Civil War History* (1991). More recently,

Michael Fellman casts a rigorously cold eye on the subject in *The Making of Robert E. Lee.*

Most of Lee's wartime letters and dispatches, personal and official, are collected in *The Wartime Papers of Robert E. Lee,* edited by Clifford Dowdey and Louis H. Manarin, and *Lee's Dispatches,* edited by Douglas Southall Freeman.

Robert E. Lee: A Life Portrait, by David J. Eicher, reproduces a wealth of photographs, paintings, and sculpture depicting Lee, his family, and other people who figured in his life. The text is also of value. Eicher almost, but not quite, persuaded me to spell Lee's mother's first name with an *e.* (It was her son's variant, followed by Fitzhugh Lee in his biography of his uncle, but not her legal name.)

For more about Lee's family, particularly his daughters, see Mary P. Coulling's *The Lee Girls.*

For multiple considerations of Lee's generalship, see Gary W. Gallagher's anthology *Lee the Soldier.*

My text cites or quotes directly from a number of other sources, including firsthand accounts of the war by Sam R. Watkins (the latest edition of whose splendid *"Company Aytch" or, A Side Show of the Big Show,* is edited and introduced by M. Thomas Inge), Robert Stiles *(Four Years Under Marse Robert),* Henry Kyd Douglas *(I Rode with Stonewall),* and Charles Minor Blackford *(Letters from Lee's Army,* compiled by Susan Leigh Bradford); the indispensable *Mary Chesnut's Civil War,* edited by C. Vann Woodward; *Thomas Morris Chester, Black Civil War Correspondent,* edited by R. J. M. Blackett; *Recollections and Letters of Robert E. Lee by His Son, Capt. Robert E. Lee;* Robert Penn Warren's *John Brown: The Making of a Martyr;* James I. Robertson Jr.'s *Stonewall Jackson: The Man, the Soldier, the Legend;* Emory Thomas's *Bold Dragoon: The Life of J. E. B. Stuart;* Bell Irvin Wiley's imperishable *The Life of Johnny Reb;* of course, Shelby Foote's *The Civil War: A Narrative;* Edmund Wilson's *Patriotic Gore; The Robert E. Lee Family Cooking and Housekeeping Book,* by Anne Carter Zimmer; *Glorious Battle: The Cultural Politics of Victorian Anglo-Catholicism,* by John Shelton Reed; *The Drama of the Gifted Child,* by Alice Miller; a collection of provocative essays entitled

The Gettysburg Nobody Knows, edited by Gabor S. Boritt; two sprightly considerations of Civil War context, Kenneth S. Greenberg's *Honor and Slavery* and Thomas P. Lowry's *The Story the Soldiers Wouldn't Tell;* and three novels: M. A. Harper's *For the Love of Robert E. Lee,* Evelyn Scott's *The Wave,* and Michael Shaara's *The Killer Angels.*

Other works that I found helpful include the following:

American Slavery, 1619–1877, by Peter Kolchin

Attack and Die: Civil War Military Tactics and the Southern Heritage, by Grady McWhiney and Perry D. Jamieson

Battle Cry of Freedom, by James M. McPherson

The Confederate War, by Gary W. Gallagher

Fields of Battle: The Wars for North America, by John Keegan

Four Years with General Lee, by Walter H. Taylor

From Manassas to Appomattox, by Gen. James Longstreet

Grant: A Biography, by William S. McFeely

Grant and Lee: A Study in Personality and Generalship, by Maj. Gen. J. F. C. Fuller

Gray Fox: Robert E. Lee and the Civil War, by Burke Davis

Lee: The Last Years, by Charles Bracelen Flood

Lee and His Generals in War and Memory, by Gary W. Gallagher

Lee's Miserables: Life in the Army of Northern Virginia from the Wilderness to Appomattox, by J. Tracy Power

The Lees of Virginia, by Paul C. Nagel

Light-Horse Harry Lee and the Legacy of the American Revolution, by Charles Royster

Memoirs of the Confederate War for Independence, by the inimitable Heros von Borcke

Military Memoirs of a Confederate, by Gen. Edward Porter Alexander

The Personal Memoirs of Julia Dent Grant, edited by John Y. Simon

Pickett's Charge, by George R. Stewart

Recollections of the Civil War, by Charles A. Dana

Reminiscences of the Civil War, by General John B. Gordon

The Rise and Fall of the American Whig Party, by Michael F. Holt

BIBLIOGRAPHY

Six Years of Hell: Harpers Ferry During the Civil War, by Chester G. Hearn
Thomas Jefferson, by Fawn M. Brodie
Ulysses S. Grant, Soldier and President, by Geoffrey Perret
The Unwritten War: American Writers and the Civil War, by Daniel Aaron
Washington: The Indispensable Man, by James Thomas Flexner